Writers in BLACK & WHITE

Contemporary authors discuss the writing life

A book by Contact Publishing

Dedicated to: To all who enjoy books, writing, and who are living the writing life in one way or another.

Contact Publishing
United Kingdom

British Library Cataloguing in Publication Data.

The interviews conducted by Alanna Lynott include
Charles Cumming; Edmund Conway; Jeffrey Lewis; Philip Hoare;
Paul Hoffman; Alex Wheatle; Hanif Kureishi;
William Coles; Stephen Benatar; Minette Walters;
Sarah Bradford; Barbara Trapido; Esther Freud; Siobhan Curham;
Simon Mawer; Ben Shephard.

The interviews conducted by Solange Berchemin include: Alex Horne; Aminatta Forna; Anna Whitelock; Brian Chikwava; Cathi Unsworth; Colin Thubron; Elizabeth Laird; Farahad Zama; Heidi Rice; Jennifer Joyce; Jim Crace; Joanne Harris; Lee Child; Nicholas Murray; Vestal McIntyre

A CIP catalogue record of this book is available from The British Library

ISBN 9781907688157

Typsetting, Book and Cover Design by Maria Rodriguez

www.contact-publishing.com

Contents

Introductions

It's mid-February. I am seated comfortably in the business lounge of the British Library about to be interviewed by Anne Mortensen, publisher and photographer. In a minute, she will describe the broad lines of a very simple project: contact contemporary writers, interview them about their writing life, their concerns, their expectations, what their sources of inspiration are and record any advice they have to offer to budding authors. Anne will take pictures, the end product will be a photo-book. I liked Anne's project, her drive, her commitment. I agree to take the commission on. After all, this should be rather easy for somebody who has worked half her life with books.

Except that I was about to enter a collider. For the next four months I would take a journey through the minds of a group of people who have one thing in common: story telling. These individuals are full to the brim with words which demand to be written down. Famous or not, writers generously gave us their time, they passed on useful tips and described the craft of writing with gripping words. Authors offered their honest views on the contemporary literary world, its metamorphoses and their concerns over the future of writers. The interviews were enlightening and edifying and I can only hope to have reported them faithfully enough so that readers will be as mesmerised as I was.

During these interviews, writers have blown away any prejudices I may have had about writing and fame. I thought that once an author attracted favourable critics, the process got easier. Instead, I learnt that the fear never goes away. As Aminatta Forna put it, 'I write with my heart in my mouth, in a state of perpetual terror that I will not be able to write another book as good as the last.'

Every single author I met is very lucid about their line of work. Writing is rewarding but being a writer is a lonely occupation which requires a lot of perseverance. It is not an easy job. Nicholas Murray told me that if offered half a chance at becoming a writer that chance should be grabbed with both hands, 'It is difficult but every job is difficult if you do it well.' Time and time again, I was told that if someone has a story to tell then it should be written down. Don't expect riches in return, though it might happen, but tell that story, use that voice of writing, make that individual journey, it is worth it.

In the making of this book, I travelled all around London and beyond. I went across many squares on the A to Z in a single journey and even reached the end of a tube line. I sat in delightful gardens, I was given a warm welcome in St Alban's Library and a cold one in noisy pubs. I drunk cappuccinos in elegant clubs and cradled polystyrene cups of coffee on public benches. My aim was to collect as wide a variety of testimonies as possible from authors writing in all sorts of genres, from romance to history. I aimed at collating a broad spectrum of views on the industry.

I learned a lot about the editorial industry. Over 100 interview invitations were sent to agents and publishers who played prevalent roles in gaining access to the authors. Throughout, I met with people concerned about their future and how digital technology will change writing. Moreover there is a general feeling that something should be done immediately about pirated downloads.

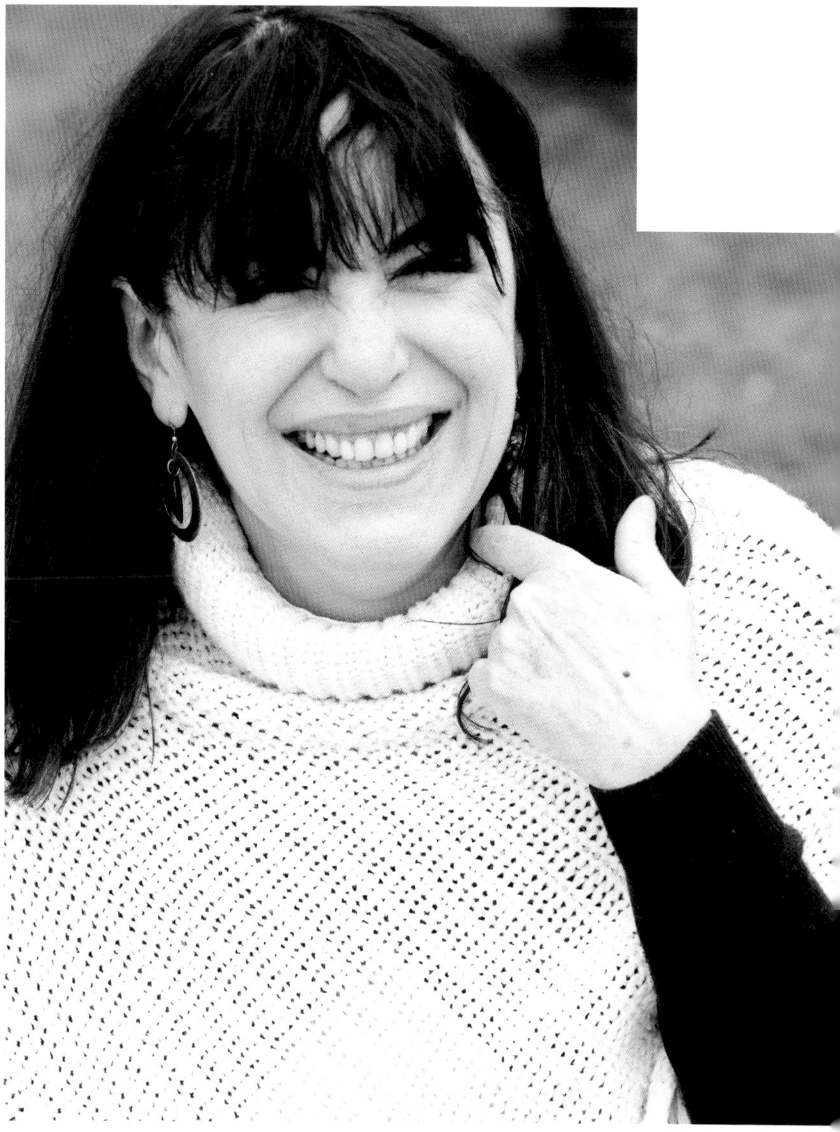

As for my own writing, the editing process taught me to cut down my "hypotyposis", and at times I even despaired. Knowing what I know now, I might take a leaf out of Alex Horne's book, metaphorically speaking, and send the discarded passages to the relevant authors.

As it is, there is nothing to change, this was an enthralling project, and the end result makes an inspirational read.

Solange Berchemin

Introductions

I, like every other self-professed 'writer' out there, have a half-written manuscript and tens of half-formed ideas lurking in my laptop, hiding in obscurely labeled files. At 26, labeling myself a writer feels uncomfortable, improbable and vaguely pretentious. To decline invitations because I'm working on 'my book' sounds absurd, and to say that the words come easily is a lie.

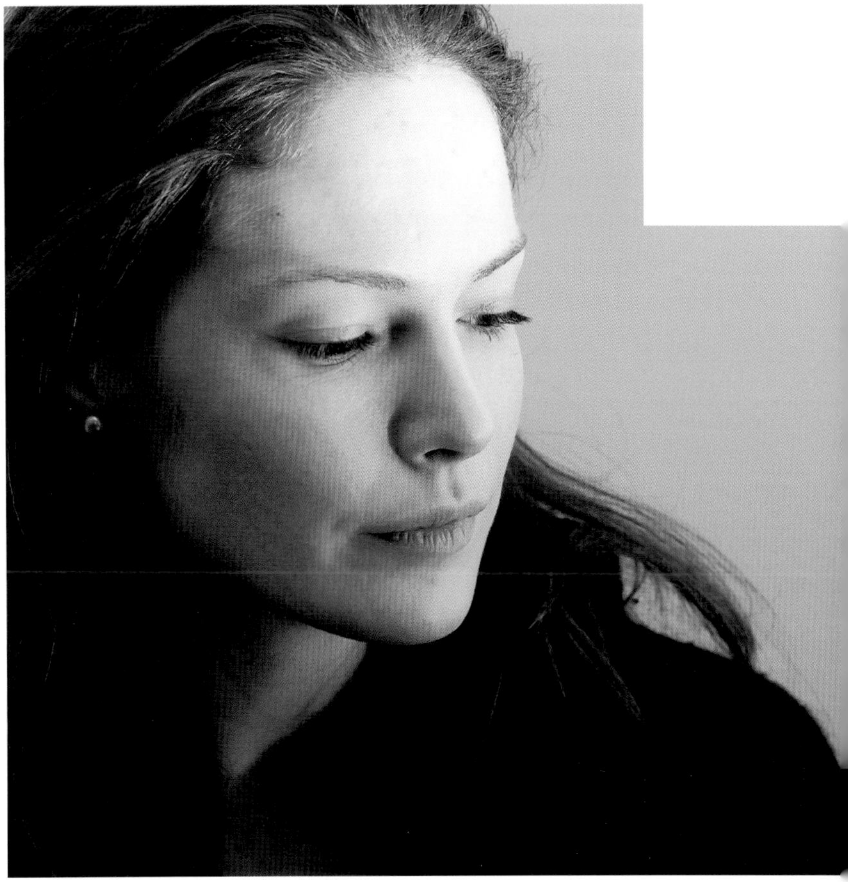

Writing is immense hard work and for a long time I worried that, because I had to spend hours twisting my sentences into shape, hammering the keyboard just to find one useable scene, and waiting for the perfect word to make its way from my head to my fingers, I was not a true writer. Luckily for me this project presented itself just in time to save my sanity. From the very first author I interviewed to the very last, each admitted openly that they found writing a difficult, often infuriating beast to wrestle with.

With relief and more than a little horribly selfish glee, I listened as Esther Freud likened writing to 'twisting metal,' as Hanif Kureishi called it a 'struggle,' as Minette Walters labeled it 'occasionally depressing' and as Simon Mawer branded it an 'awful, boring, solitary grind.' I was glad to hear that these world-renowned authors found it hard. I was also glad to know that it wasn't just me.

Of course, once your manuscript is complete the hard part begins. Grabbing and holding on to the attention of an agent and a publisher is notoriously difficult. But, according to the majority of the writers I interviewed for this book, it's a relative walk in the park compared to what comes next. By far the biggest complaint I heard (other than how poorly paid writers are of course!) was against the publicity and marketing departments of the publishing houses. Although, as Ben Shephard acknowledged, the publicists are horribly over worked, many believe they have too much power. Some feel they don't give enough support and several think they ask too much. It was a revelation for which I was not prepared. I also discovered that getting published was not the final hurdle, but rather the beginning of yet another long hard slog. It was a little daunting. However, every single one of the writers I talked to are still writers. They haven't been put off by the disappointments, the rejections or the pitfalls of the writer's life. Writing a book is worth all of that and more, and holding a published copy in your hands keeps you going all the way through to the next one.

Four words that every single author uttered to me were 'I've been very lucky.' Personally, I think luck has little to do with it; successful authors work hard and, quite simply, they're good at what they do. But it's nice to know that the writer's life, despite all signs to the contrary, is one to be thankful for. And who knows, one day I might just be lucky enough to find out.

Alanna Lynott

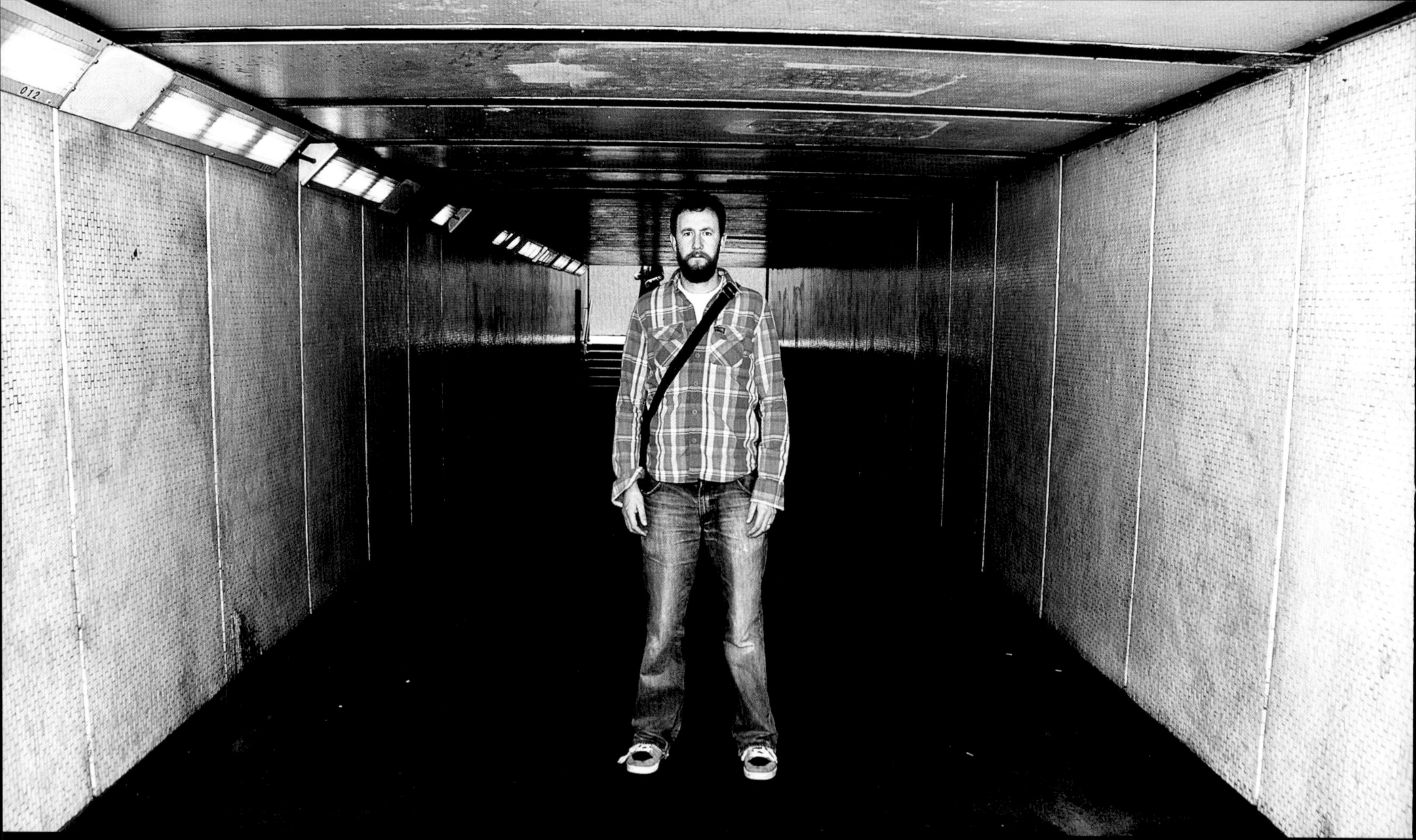

Alex Horne

SHOWS

- Word Watching (2009)
- Bird Watching (2007)
- Making Fish Laugh (2003)
- How to Avoid Huge Ships (2000)
- We Need Answers (BBC Four)

BOOKS

- Wordwatching: Breaking into the Dictionary - It's His Word Against Theirs (2009)
- Birdwatchingwatching: One Year, Two Men, Three Rules, Ten

Comedian Alex Horne devotes some of his spare time to pursuing obscure quests. His current Long Live Alex Campaign, for instance, supports his self-described 'death-defying' attempt to be the oldest man in the world. Horne also spent a year trying to out-birdwatch his father; the experience formed the basis of his Edinburgh Festival show, Bird Watching, and his first book, *Birdwatchingwatching: One Year, Two Men, Three Rules, Ten Thousand Birds.* His second book, *Wordwatching*, charts his hilarious quest to get an invented word into the dictionary.

Although he had thought for a while about writing a book, Alex Horne never got round to putting a synopsis together until a publisher's agent approached him at the Edinburgh Fringe. 'The Edinburgh Festival is really important for comedians,' he says, 'but I did not realise until afterwards how lucky I was to have been offered, on the spot, a deal for two books - though it felt a little bit like cheating because I had already written the show and the first book was going to be an extension of that.'

Being a prolific writer, the award-winning comedian set to the task with great enthusiasm. For his first draft of *Birdwatchingwatching*, he wrote five times the allocated word content. 'My first book was linked to my dad. I had written some passages specifically for him and when they were - quite rightly - left out during editing, I gathered all the cuts together and sent them to him.'

Having written books, stand-up comedy, and TV and radio material, Alex Horne is well-versed in the requirements of writing for various formats. For books, he says, authors should write first and edit later. 'I was once told, "As you are writing, don't worry about the word count" – if you feel the material should be there, write it. Then cut, cut, cut.'

Writing for TV is different from writing for publication. 'At the beginning,' he explains, 'you have no idea what you are doing, so you just do what you are told. It is very prescriptive.' He continues, 'that's how I did it, but it was wrong. If you show a bit of originality and drop the brief, TV people will be happy to take what you have produced. And if they don't, you have to tell yourself that it's not the end of the world. So my advice would be: write what you like.'

In contrast to print and TV, says the comedian, radio has the advantage of being non-visual. 'You are not limited by what people can see,' he explains. 'There is more focus on the words, but people can imagine things more on the radio. There is more potential for creativity.'

Despite his involvement with various projects, Horne still finds time to perform regularly in top comedy clubs – and, unlike some comedians, writes his own jokes. 'People don't realise it, but comedy is heavily scripted.' In fact, at the start of his career, he wrote for others; 'I was not very good at it,' he says with a smile. However, success came once he began writing his own material.

Although some of his material comes from real-life observations, much of it involves studious research and complicated psychological theories about what makes people (and sometimes fish) laugh. 'I enjoy research' he explains, 'for comedy, you are reading and learning a lot, but mainly you are watching out for very small things that are funny or details that have not been covered yet. It's like panning for gold; you are looking for little nuggets that will be interesting.'

At this stage in his career, Alex has developed an instinct for what sort of material works or doesn't work, even if it takes time to arrive at that decision. For instance, after playing golf with his father-in-law for six months, he knew that the subject matter was not universal enough for his show or his writing. However, the experience led him to research old board games and sports, which in turn became a BBC Four documentary, something that he hopes to do more of in the future.

Though he is now an acclaimed performer, there were hard times along the way. His advice is, 'write for things that you are interested in and have confidence in what you write. Be prepared, it takes years.'

What's next for Alex Horne in terms of books? 'I have two or three ideas for fiction. I am aware that it is not going to be as easy to find a publisher for a novel as it was for non-fiction.' Although he doesn't have a synopsis ready yet, he seems optimistic about his upcoming work. 'I might just write the whole manuscript and send it to publishers. In a way, I am quite looking forward to the rejections.' ■

http://www.alexhorne.com/

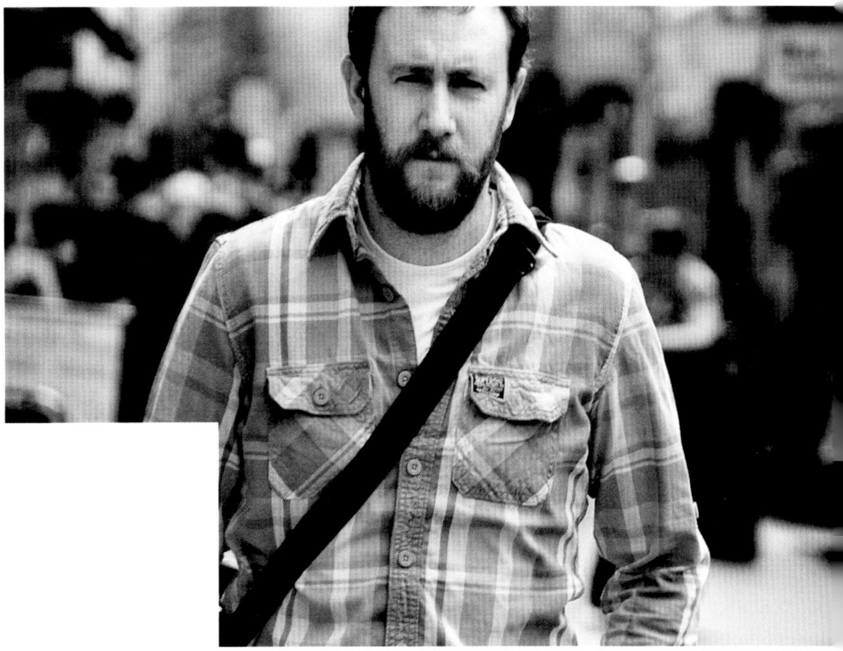

Alex Wheatle

NOVELS

- Brenton Brown (2010)
- The Dirty South (2008)
- Island Songs (2005)
- Checkers (2003)
- The Seven Sisters (2002)
- East of Acre Lane (2001)
- Brixton Rock (1999)

To hear Alex Wheatle talk of his childhood, you might think it was just like anyone else's: he was always out and about, playing football and cricket or making his own entertainment. So it comes as a shock when he reveals he spent almost his entire childhood in a children's home.

The man now known as the 'Brixton Bard,' a man with an MBE for services to literature and six books to his name, lived in government care between the ages of three and fourteen after his parents returned to Jamaica, leaving him behind in London. 'Growing up without parents, wondering where they were, why I was just left on my own - that deeply affected me,' Wheatle says. 'I didn't even know the story of my young life until I was a teenager. I just wasn't told.'

He grew up an angry and disillusioned young man and was expelled from school at the age of fifteen. 'I had a very hard time adjusting to an environment where most of the students had normal family backgrounds,' he explains. 'And the teachers just saw an angry black kid. They didn't dig deep to see what I was all about and they didn't understand.'

Despite all this, there is no trace of anger in Wheatle's soft voice, nor is there any indication that he's driven by a search for pity or the desire to shock. Perhaps this is due in part to the passing of time and the dulling of pain, but he himself credits the power of music, particularly reggae, for this aspect of his personality.

At the age of 15 Alex was living in a Social Services hostel in Brixton, where he was 'more or less a street kid' involved in petty crime and drug dealing, which led to a short stint in Wormwood Scrubs. 'I had no sense of belonging,' he says. 'I felt my life was basically rubbish; I had no aspirations at all. I never thought I could contribute in any way to society and some days I was suicidal because I felt there was no life for me, no happy life.'

1970s Brixton was a volatile area of London, rife with racial tension and unemployment, but it also had its charms. While not exactly comparable to Jamaica's Kingston, Brixton pulsed with a heady Afro-Caribbean beat. Locals had their own way of speaking, walking and dancing, making it a unique place at that moment in time. 'Music was everywhere,' Wheatle recalls. 'It had such a strong influence and reggae music politicised me before I even knew what that meant. It became a kind of teacher for me.'

In those days, MCs and DJs were the champions of the area - local news reporters and social commentators rolled into one - and Wheatle wanted that life, and after a shaky start, 'Yardman Irie' was born. 'I used to write lyrics every day,' Wheatle says. 'My grammar may not have been too good but at least I was aspiring to be someone; I was expressing myself. Everything I had in me for all those years, I could get it out of my system.'

By the mid-1980s, Wheatle's lyrics notepad was several inches thick, so he had a lot to draw on when he finally decided to write a book. However, he was initially reluctant to start. 'I shied away from

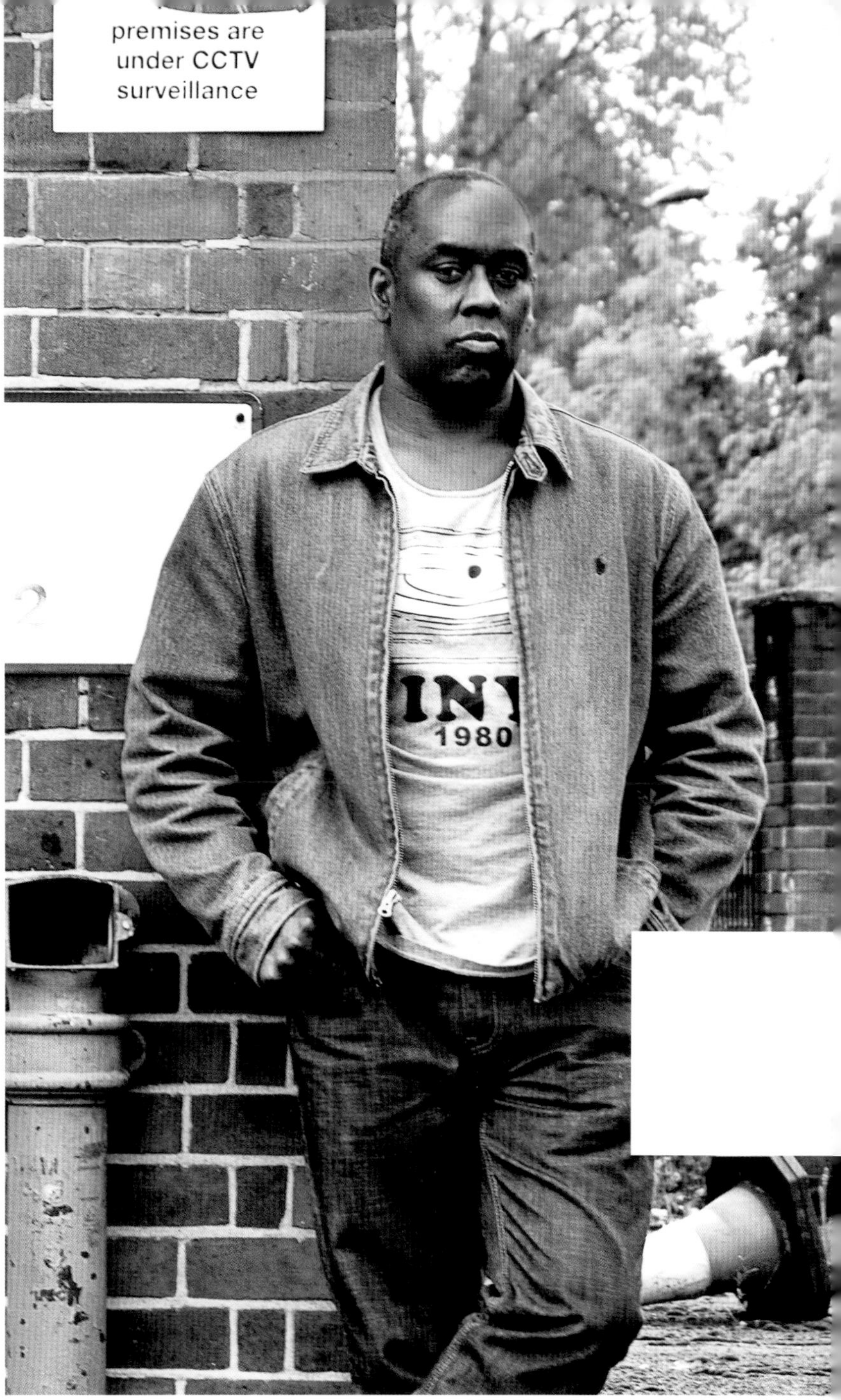

it for a long while because I thought people would laugh at my attempts,' he says. But his friends kept encouraging him, and eventually he wrote his first novel *Brixton Rock*, in which he describes his experiences, along with those of his friends, of growing up alone in the world. 'It took a long while,' Wheatle remembers, 'because I didn't really know what I was doing. I knew the story I wanted to tell but I didn't know how to formulate it. It was really just emotion on the page.'

Now Alex works out the story in his head before he starts to write. 'Before I've even got any notes or any characters I try to work ▶

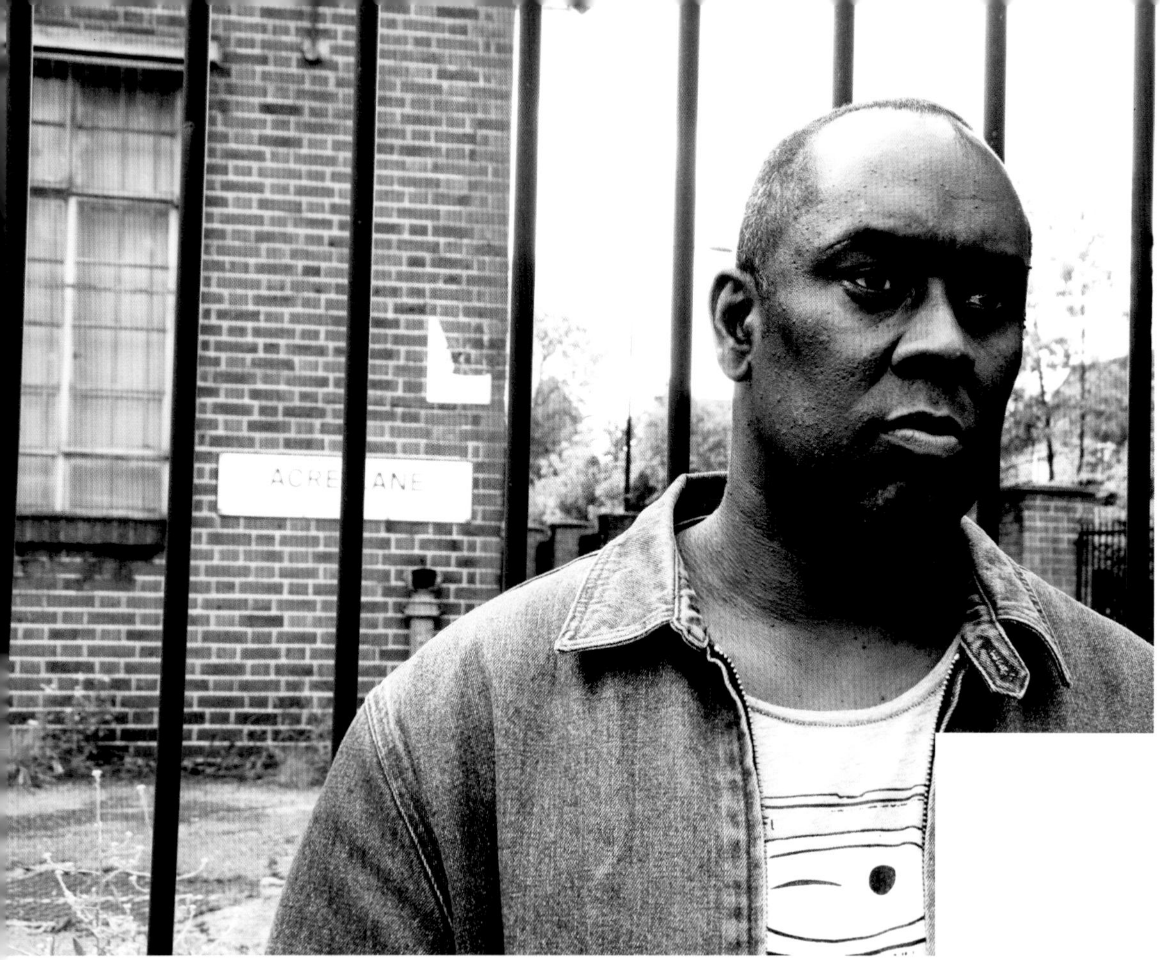

out a vague ending.' He advises budding writers to think of it like driving a car in the dark. 'Say you want to get from London to Leeds,' he says. 'You can't see Leeds but you know it's there somewhere, you know it's north. So that's how I think of my endings: I know it's north, I know it's that way and I just try to get there.'

Once *Brixton Rock* was finally finished, Alex looked up the biggest agent he could find in the local library's copy of The Writer's and Artist's Yearbook and personally delivered his handwritten, cigarette-burned manuscript to their office. 'I was very confident,' he says. 'I thought I was going to make a million pounds.' The agent merely asked if he had a typed copy and Wheatle asked them if they would type it up – you can imagine the reply. Crushed, he went home and abandoned the book for over a year.

However, he eventually bought a secondhand typewriter and taught himself to type. 'You don't want to know how long it took to type it all out,' he says. 'Put it this way: I think in the first night I only typed the title.'

Despite sending the manuscript out to over twenty agents and publishers and receiving no replies, he refused to be cowed. '[I thought,] what are they thinking?' he says. 'To me it was a masterpiece – the best thing since Oliver Twist!' That attitude saved Wheatle from giving up and missing out on hearing back from Black Amber, the small publishing house that printed *Brixton Rock.*

He's not ashamed to say that to hold the book in his hands for the first time brought a tear to his eye. 'It was incredible,' he says. 'It really shouted out to all those doubters in my young life who said I was rubbish. It was the proudest experience of my life.'

To get to this point, Wheatle advises that you must write everyday. 'Just get into the habit of writing,' he says. 'The more you write, the better you get. Someone once said to write a good word, you have to write 100,000 bad ones and I think that's true to an extent. Just write something everyday – even if it's just a sentence and then it won't be so daunting when you come to actually sit down and write your book.

Wheatle has since established relationships with his father, who lives in Jamaica, and his mother, who lives in America. 'Half of *Brixton Rock* is about scenarios that happened in my life and it's hard for my father to take. There's a lot of guilt there, because ultimately he's the one that gave me up,' Wheatle admits. 'But in 2000, I went over to Jamaica when the book was launched there; my father came to the events and it was such a proud moment for us both.'.

Wheatle still has friends who never found their families, and feels immensely grateful that he managed to do so. 'Sometimes you don't get surprise endings – but you get an understanding. I don't want to be pitied; I just feel lucky that I've managed to have a relationship with my parents and forge a career for myself. It's been fantastic.' ■

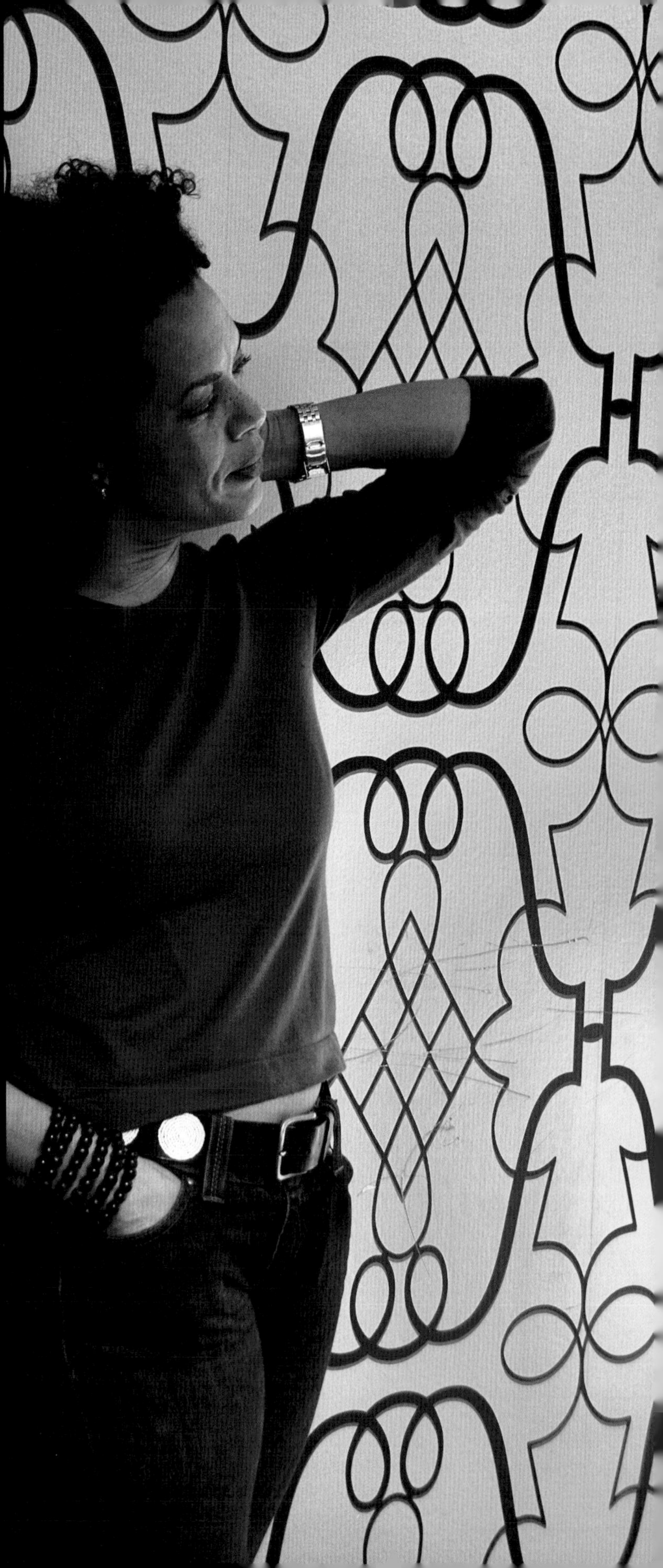

Aminatta Forna

NOVELS

- The Memory of Love (2010)
- Ancestor Stones (2006)
- The Devil that Danced on the

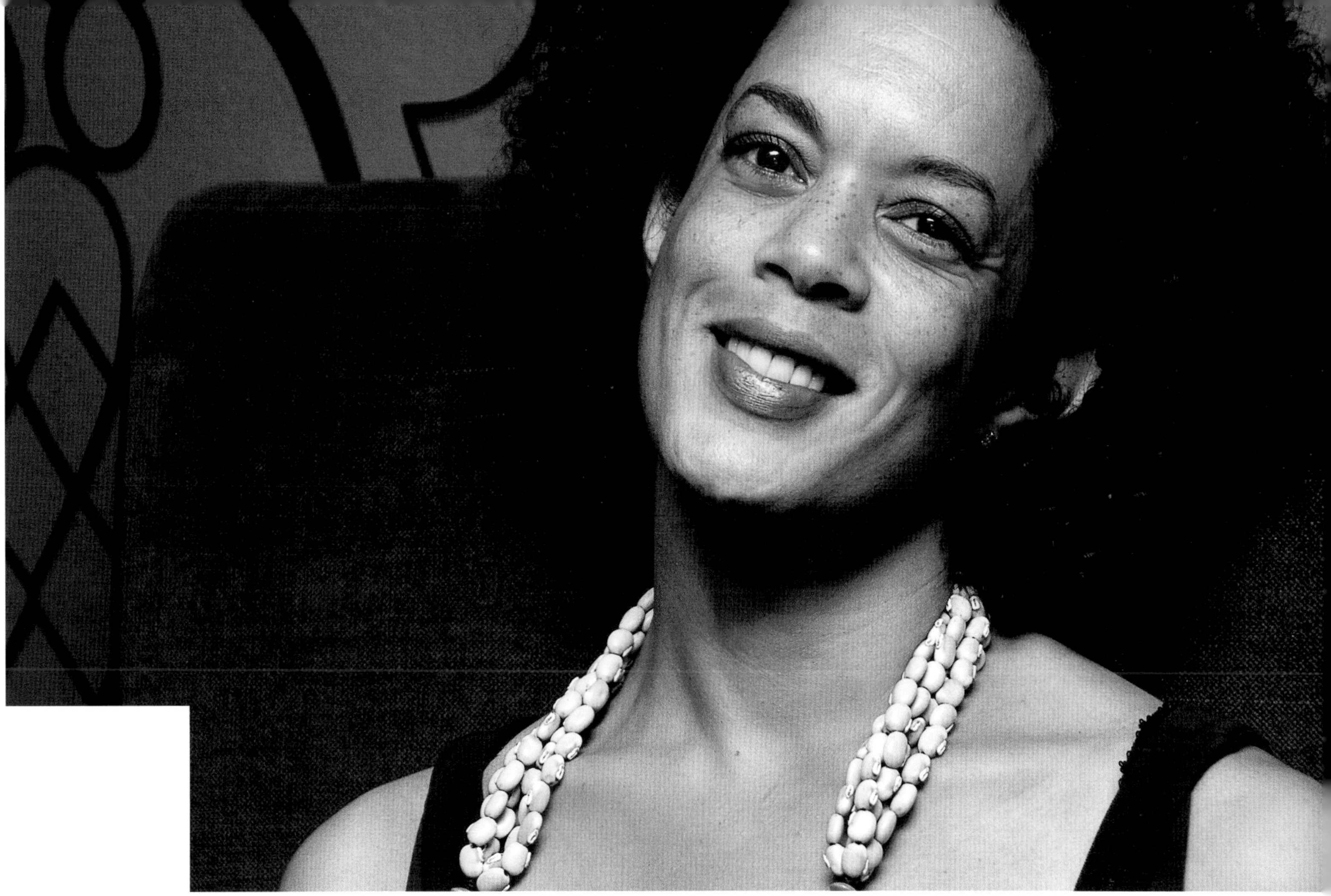

The Memory of Love, the latest novel from Sierra Leonean-Scottish writer Aminatta Forna, received rave reviews. The Guardian's reviewer concluded her article with 'This is a remarkable novel... the kind that deserves to be on the Booker shortlist.'

Forna's debut as a professional author came at the cost of a high-paying position as a BBC journalist. Why did she leave behind the security of her job for the precarious livelihood of full-time writing?

'It was a career decision,' she says. 'By the time I finished my first book, I was in debt. Most people are after the first book. You need the stomach and the endurance for it, and you have to be prepared to quit your day job and be poor. Only another artist or somebody who has done it can understand.'

With the benefit of hindsight, she gives an astute depiction of the situation. 'You have to think about it like starting a business. Would you expect to make a profit in the first two months? Of course not. You would write a five-year business plan and give the business time; and during that time, you would have to mortgage your house and pour your savings into the venture. That is exactly what it is like with writing, and during that time, you have no guarantee that you are going to be a successful writer or even a working writer.'

Forna feels that her noticeably detailed writing, with its emphasis on accurate descriptions and precise scenes, has been influenced by her previous career. 'Journalism is not like writing a book at all, and certainly not like writing a novel. But I did learn a certain craft from journalism. I certainly learned how to do research and the value of it, and that it is not worth faking it. I give six months to a year to research, then I get enough of "the bits" and I can begin.'

However, Forna has found that research alone cannot shape a book. 'In the course of writing, the book will change in quite a lot of ways.' This is another lesson learned from journalism. 'To hone the idea of what a story is, even if the story is 300 words, journalists have to find an interesting way of telling people the things they want to tell.' While research is important to the writing process, Forna's inspiration often comes from what she feels and hears. 'It is usually not conscious,' she says. 'This book, *The Memory of Love*, ▶

started with what somebody told me in 1999, before I had even written the other two books. That idea came back and came back until one day I thought, that's what I want to write.'

Once a year, Forna teaches a creative writing course at Goldsmiths College, which has given her new insight into common mistakes made by beginners. 'They don't know what their story is and it goes off on a tangent, becoming very unwieldy. As a journalist you always know that a story has a line. You can always depart from that line but you have to remember where the line is. When you don't have that, you have to work much harder on always knowing where the line of your story is.'

Different writers, she believes, will encounter different hurdles during their individual careers depending on, '...what kind of writing you want to do and what kind of writer you are capable of becoming. Being a commercial writer is different from being a literary writer. With the former the reader wants to get into a certain rhythm, and that's not a bad thing - there are other books that are here to surprise and challenge.'

Over the course of writing three books, Forna has discovered the two most crucial relationships for writers. 'The editor is the second most important person, and the most important relationship you have is with your agent.' Her agent, she says, is the person to whom she owes her entire career. 'My agent thinks about his clients: where their career is going and where they want to go.

Before anything else you need an agent. An agent is somebody who fights for you, defends you and reads every single word you have written. There are also agents who do nothing but get you the biggest advance they can, and that is fine if it is what you need.'

Another key relationship for writers, Forna continues, is the one they have with their publisher. 'Whether an author wants a small publisher or a large publisher is entirely up to the individual. A small one is much more convivial; writers know who is looking after them, and they will have the opportunity to chat with the publicist and the editor when they need to. A big publisher has a lot more money to put behind a book, both in terms of advance and publicity.'

Forna leaves me with some words of encouragement for nervous writers. 'Like every writer I know, I write with my heart in my mouth, in a state of perpetual terror. I don't know anybody who has done it differently. I think if you are too confident, this is a sign that something is wrong. Confidence comes from the fact that it has been okay before, so you pray that it will be okay again. I don't think the angst ever goes away - nor should it,' she concludes. 'It keeps you alive, and it means that you are testing the boundaries of creativity.' ■

http://www.aminattaforna.com/

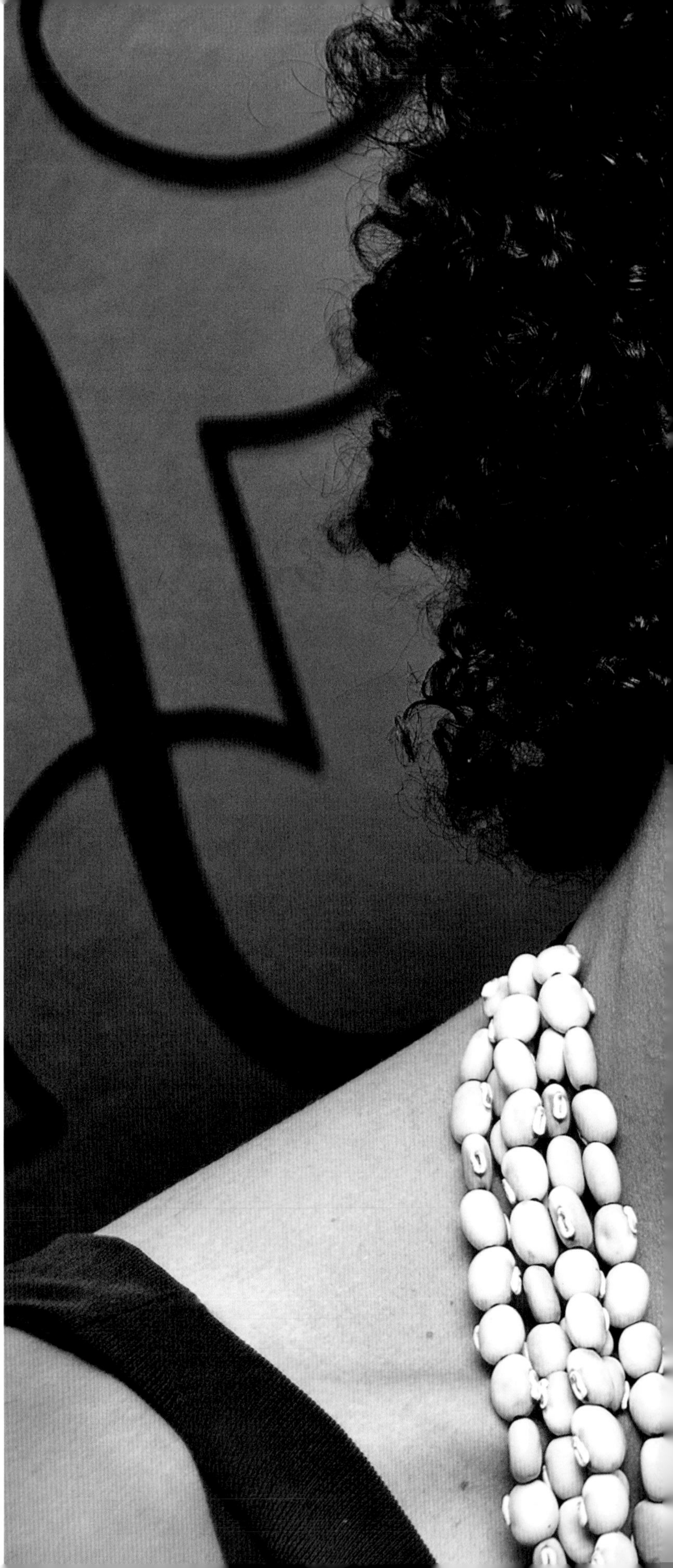

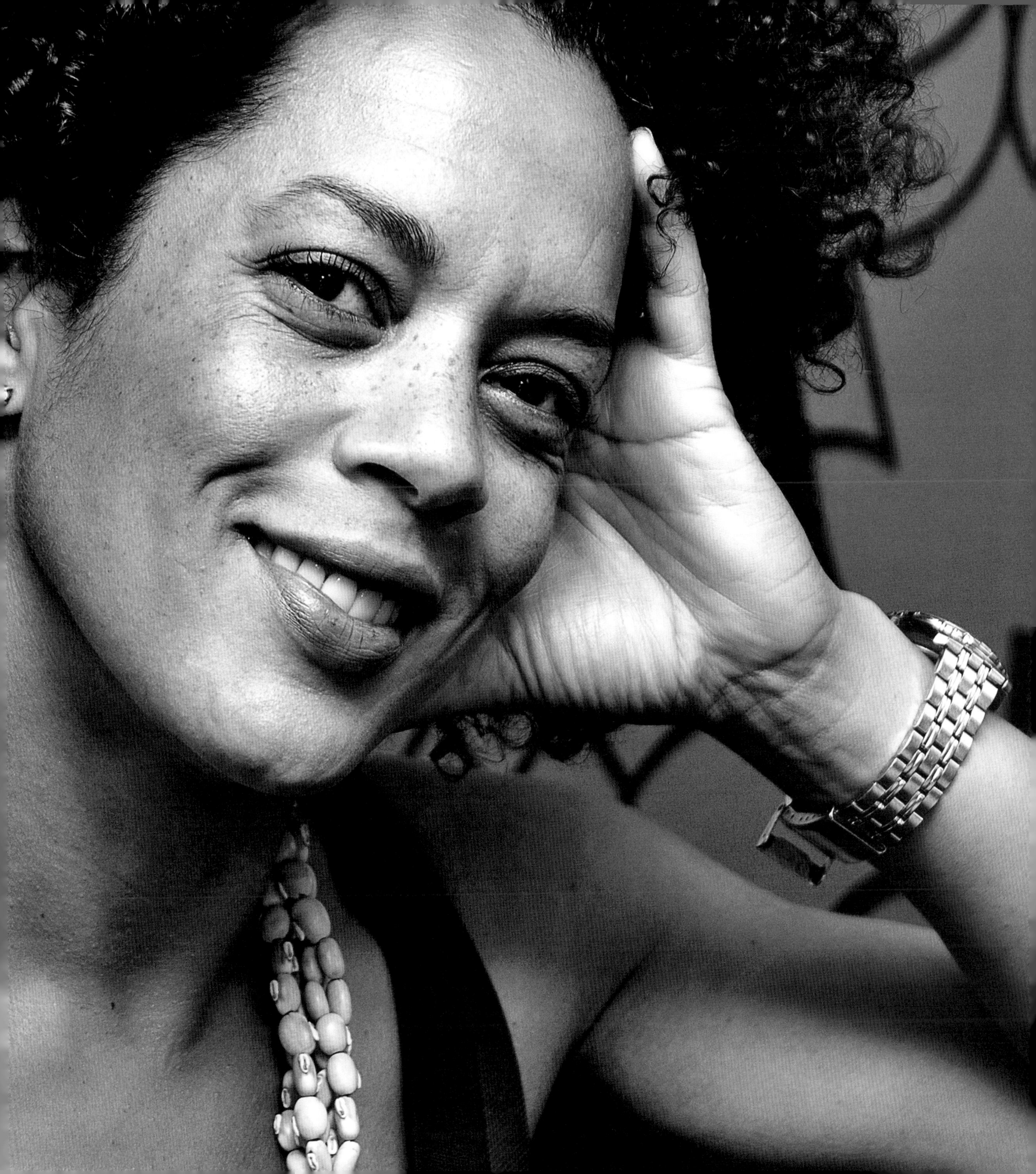

Cathy Unsworth

NOVELS

- Bad Penny Blues (2009)
- The Singer (2007)
- The Not Knowing (2005)

SHORT STORY COLLECTION

- London Noir: Capital Crime Fiction (2006) (as editor)

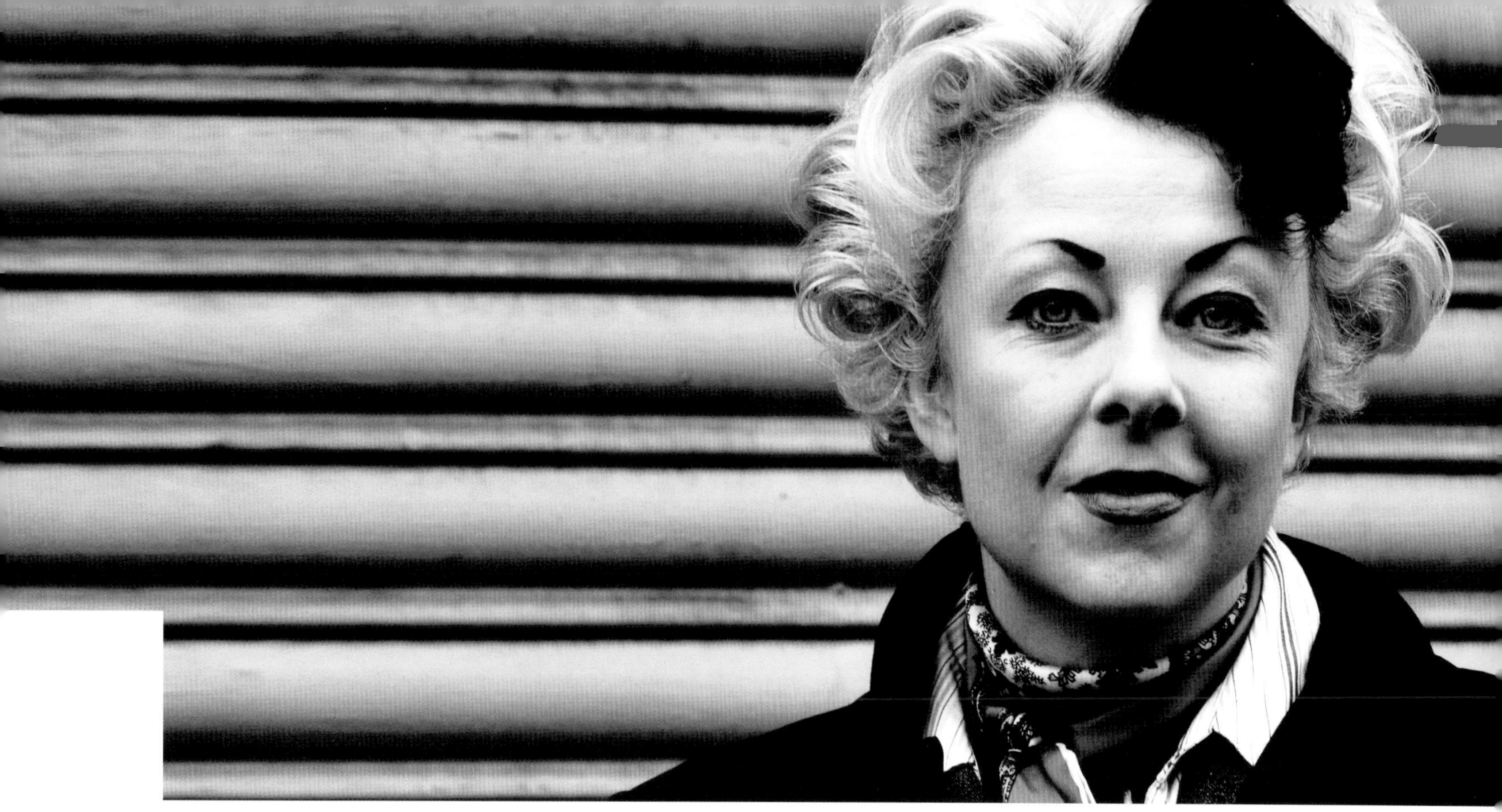

At the age of 19, Cathi Unsworth, still at art college, walked (though I suspect she waltzed) into the offices of the legendary music magazine, *Sounds*, which was at the forefront of covering the punk movement. Her sole intent was to prove to the editor of this publication, whom she so admired, that she was the new recruit he didn't know he needed.

About a decade later, Cathi Unsworth had interviewed all the artists she wanted to. Moreover, the music scene was now changing very quickly, with all the marginal little bands she liked being pushed out of the way by groups such as Oasis and Blur.

Not very long before, she had interviewed British crime fiction author Derek Raymond, the founder of the English noir genre. Raymond had gained fame in France, where 'polars' or 'romans policiers' are readers' staple diet. Cathi Unsworth had no idea that crime fiction could be like that: stories that got under the skin, analyses of how crime affects people, with a viewpoint other than that of the clever detective - in Monsieur Raymond's words, 'romans noir versus entertainment fiction.' Influenced by his work, Cathi applied herself to the genre.

'An editor told me that if I had changed my name to a man's name,' the author recalls, 'I would have had no problem finding a big publisher.' We ponder over this for a little while, discuss it briefly, turn it round and round for the time it deserves and quickly brush it away.

As far as she is concerned, choosing a good publisher is crucial. She explains that nowadays, publishing is a bit like the record industry: 'They sign you for one record, or in this case, one book, and that's it.' Some publishers even go so far as to tell their authors what to write; a friend of Unsworth's was asked "to kill her favourite character". Cathi Unsworth is vehement that a writer should not have to compromise. Unlike her friend, she has managed to find a nurturing publisher in Serpent's Tail. The firm, which Cathi affectionately calls her 'Addams family,' has published all of her novels, as well as the short story compendium which she edited. Serpent's Tail is also set to publish her upcoming novel, which takes place in Norfolk where she grew up.

When Cathi Unsworth first did live readings, she was afraid of being that mumbling person in the corner. However, her friends helped her to project herself. Did she find her inner luvvie then? I get my answer in the form of an infectious giggle.

She proceeds to tell me about her appearance at Avant! Noir, a night of the London Word Festival which includes animation, jazz, readings and more, and about 'Transmission,' a collaboration between herself and electronic composer Pete Woodhead. This latter project led to an invitation from NRK Radio to come to Oslo and start an initiative for writers and musicians to work together on similar collaborations. That's what's great about Cathi Unsworth: she's an author with a book bug, and if you get near her or one of her books, you might just catch it too. ■

For more on Cathi Unsworth, visit: http://www.cathiunsworth.com/

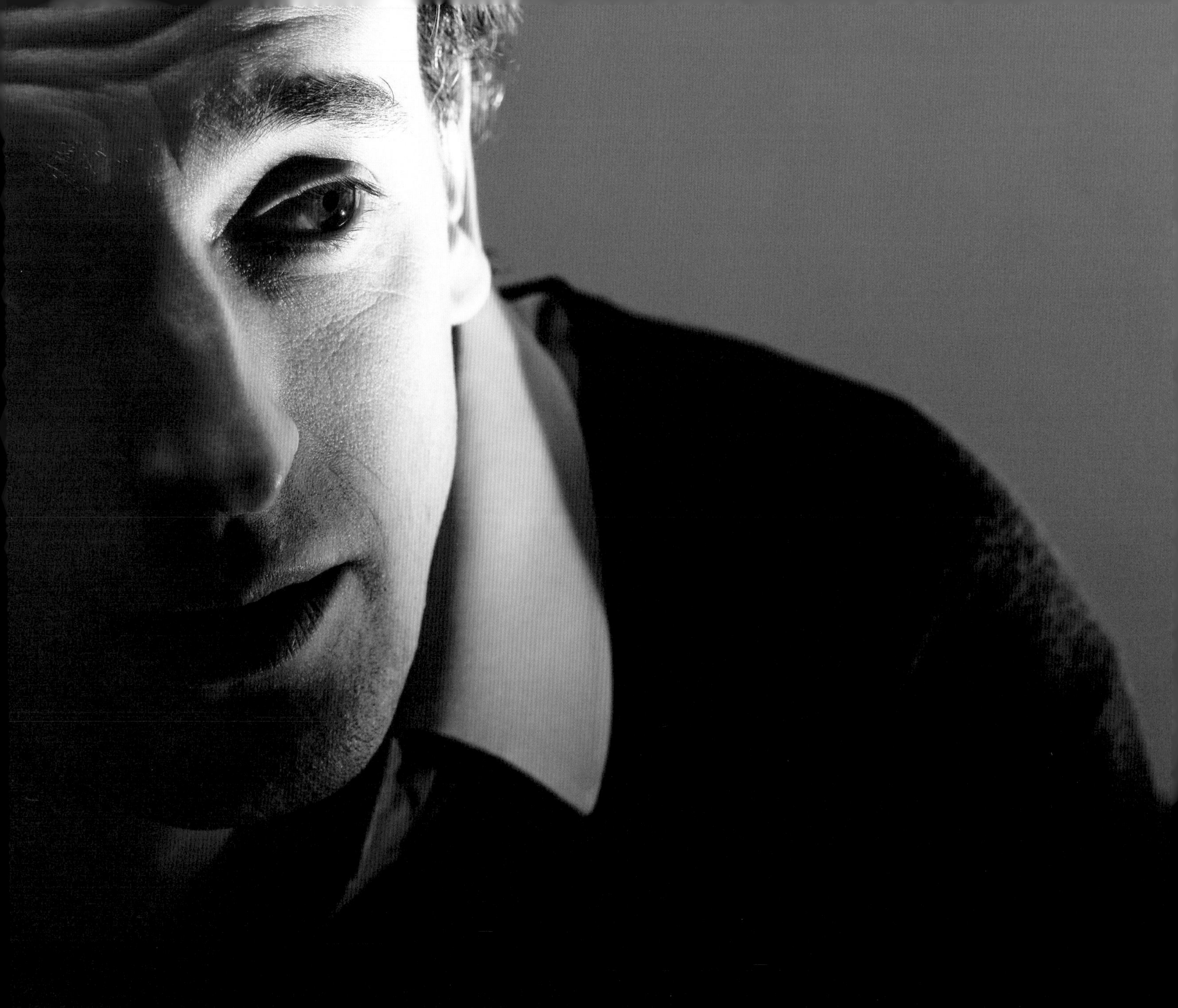

Charles Cumming

NOVELS

- The Trinity Six (2011)
- Typhoon(2008)
- The Spanish Game(2006)
- The Hidden Man(2003)
- A Spy by Nature(2001)

Charles Cumming freely admits that he isn't an alpha-male type - and thank goodness for that, for if he were as ruthless as the spies that inhabit his books, he might never have become a writer. When Cumming was 25, fresh out of university and trying to decide what to do with his life, a chance meeting at a dinner party led to an invitation to try out for MI6.

'An old family friend had just retired from the Foreign Office and moved to the area, so my stepfather invited him over for supper,' he recalls. 'It was the night that Yitzhak Rabin was assassinated. Perhaps our friend thought my observations were insightful because a couple of days later, he bumped into my mother and asked whether I'd ever thought about joining the Foreign Office.' At the time, Cumming was working as a waiter in Fulham and toying with the idea of getting into journalism; he didn't expect to learn in his Foreign Office interview that he had been talent-spotted by MI6. 'I was very surprised,' he says, 'that they had seen something in me that could make me suited to a life as a professional liar. I had quite a limited view of espionage at the time – and I was too young, far too young.'

After the initial conversation, more tests, trials and interviews followed, and although Cumming didn't make it through, the seed of a story was planted. 'I don't know why I didn't get in,' he says. 'I suspect it was because I had a tendency to joke my way out of things. If you're going to be an MI6 officer you've got to be really serious, with a spine of steel and a core ruthlessness that I lack.'

But his experience was crying out to be dramatised. 'It was very obvious. I'd always wanted to write a book and this just fell into my lap.' And so the idea for Cumming's debut novel, *A Spy by Nature*, was born from the twists and turns that his life might have taken had he joined MI6.

He moved to Montreal for four months and began writing the book (ostensibly, he says, to impress his then-girlfriend, now his wife). Cumming admits he had no idea what he was doing, but that the book was all the better for it. 'I was free to do what I wanted so it's quite an unusual spy thriller in its structure and in terms of character. There isn't all that much wham-bam action, but I think that's its greatest strength.'

Work on *A Spy by Nature* began at the end of 1996, but the first draft wasn't completed until the spring of 1999. 'It's all the cogitation, all the marinating of the ideas - I really believe you have to wait for it to come, you can't force it,' says Cumming.

Although the writing process was slow, the process of getting published was lightning-fast. A friend of Cumming's who was a literary agent read the manuscript and sold it to Penguin. 'Getting published was actually really easy,' Cumming tells me with a sheepish look. 'I don't have a struggle story - it's really embarrassing!'

However, he assures me that successful publication didn't ensure smooth sailing. 'What you discover is that getting published is the least of your problems. It's an amazingly crowded and tremendously competitive, ruthless environment and there's very little money spent on advertising or marketing.'

'You get spoiled as a first novelist. That's certainly what happened to me,' Cumming recalls. 'I was on the radio, the front cover of the Times, and I was thinking, This is a breeze. Then with the second and third books, nada! And it's because they've told your story and the market likes new blood. It feasts on the young and attractive,' he adds with a grimace. Cumming tries to promote his work at every opportunity, using Facebook and Twitter – even rearranging bookshop displays so his book is where it's supposed to be. 'We have to dash into every bookshop we pass – it's the bane of my wife's life,' he laughs.

Looking back, he believes he was very lucky to get into writing when he did, as he feels there's no real chance for authors to develop their careers anymore. 'It's two strikes and you're out,' he says. 'If you get a two-book deal for your debut novel, the debut novel or the follow-up has got to earn its money back or you're out. It's horrible and depressing and very bad for the writing culture.'

It also scares Cumming that writers are required to write faster and faster in order to maintain their place in the shops and their relationship with the publishers. 'The faster you're required to go, there's no doubt at all in my mind that the quality of the work will eventually suffer.' As someone who has to really force himself to write, this worries Cumming. 'I'm not a writer who just sits down and the words just fall from my fingers.' However, he believes that writer's block is a self-fulfilling prophecy. 'It's the Macbeth of the literary world,' he states, 'in that you avoid saying it or thinking about it. You can get yourself into a tailspin about it, when in fact all you really need is to wait.'

Despite all the negatives, it's clear that Cumming loves what he does, but his one piece of advice to anyone who wants to follow the same path is to have another job – 'otherwise,' he says, 'you won't be able to pay your way, especially as you get older. That's really hard to hear as a 24-year-old – it's counter-intuitive to pursuing your dream. You should pursue your dream, but with a footnote. And if you want to write, there's really nothing stopping you in this country – try writing in China or Iran.' ■

Find out more at www.charlescumming.co.uk

Barbara Trapido

NOVELS

- Sex & Stravinsky (2010)
- Frankie & Stankie (2003)
- The Travelling Hornplayer (1998)
- Juggling (1994)
- Temples of Delight (1990)
- Noah's Ark (1984)
- Brother of the More Famous Jack (1982)

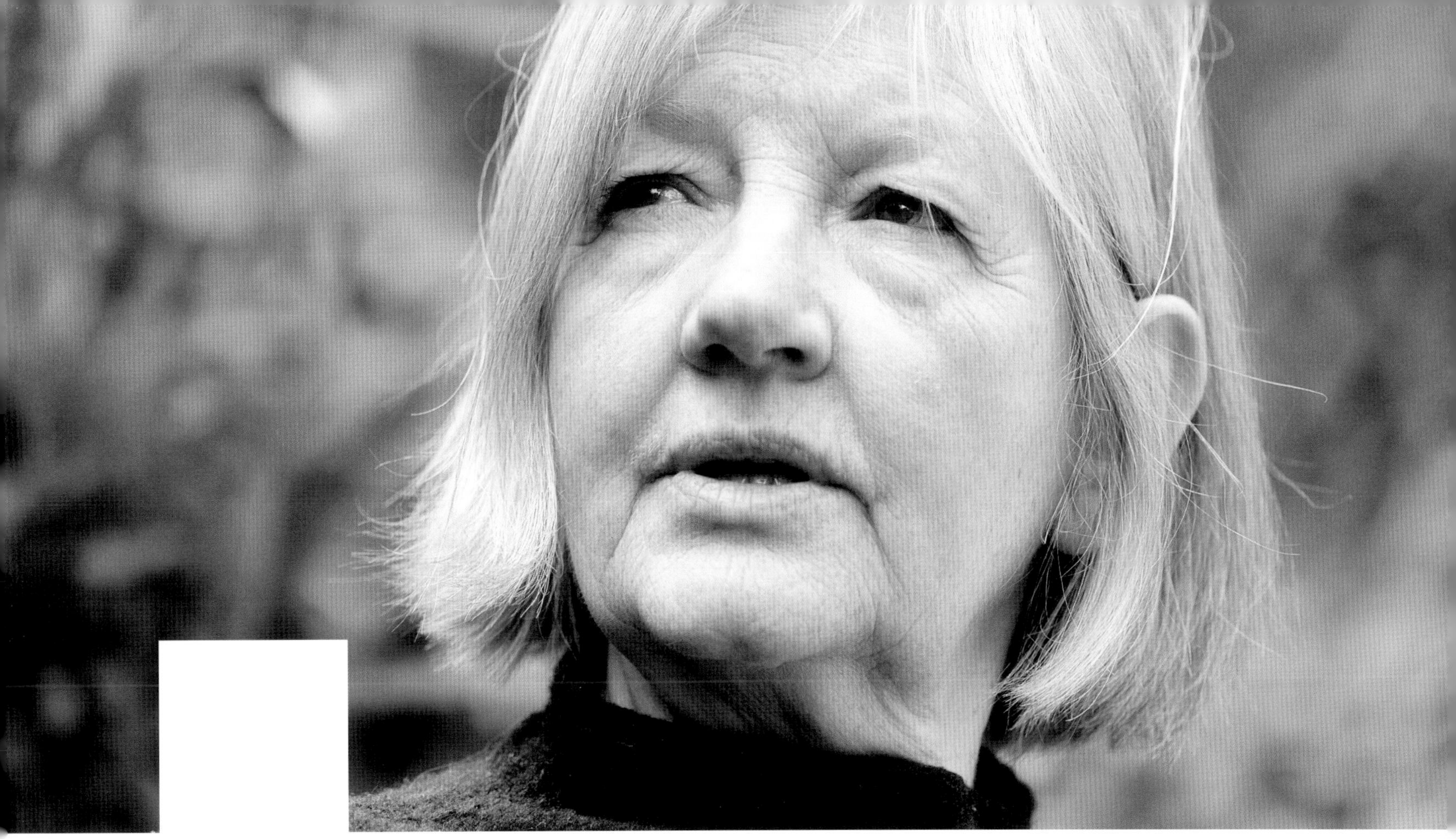

Barbara Trapido's relatively easy entrée into the publishing world heralded the beginning of a long and successful career as a novelist. And yet, strangely, she never had any ambition to be a writer.

Growing up in South Africa, Trapido found it to be the perfect place for a 'little girl who liked day-dreaming and playing by herself,' with trees to climb and bamboo grasses to hide in while she invented characters in her head. She found school difficult because, in her words, 'I was a very clingy, mummy-ish sort of girl and school was a big shock,' full of 'very strict, very white' teachers. To escape, she 'endlessly' wrote little poems, plays and stories such as 'The Strange Little Dog Who Only Ate Tomatoes,' an early indication of her whimsical imagination.

After university, where she studied English Literature, Trapido got married and moved to England with her husband in the 1960s. Although still a daydreamer, she no longer wrote down her stories. It wasn't until a friend, growing tired of watching Trapido dissipate her talent by telling stories at dinner parties, begged her to write a short story for the Guardian Short Story competition. 'So I started,' she recalls, 'and I dreamed up a family of characters, but after a while I thought, I don't want to write a short story, I just want to follow these people around and let them develop' - which she did, before life got in the way and she stuffed her notes away in a drawer for the next ten years.

Trapido didn't look at the notes again until another friend urged her to pick up where she left off. She 'started daydreaming about it,' although with a part-time teaching job and a house full of children, she rarely got the chance to write down any of her thoughts. 'I found I was living more and more in my head,' she remembers. 'I wasn't really writing much down in those days. I was just having dialogues in my head and I got very addicted to it. I thought maybe I was going mad, talking to these people who weren't real.'

Eventually, however, the story demanded to be written. 'I didn't have a plot; I just had this group of people who would sort of bounce off each other,' Trapido says. 'I started off writing and I discovered the pleasure of it came from the tunes you could make with the language, and then I got really obsessed with writing it down. We usually had about three houseguests at any one time and I couldn't wait for them to go to bed so I could talk to those imaginary people instead.'

With no one standing over her demanding the manuscript by a certain date, Trapido relished taking as long as she needed to. Fortified with black coffee, she would sit up night after night, typing on a little Olivetti. Not being aware of the existence of literary agents, Trapido stuck her manuscript into an envelope and sent it out to two ▶

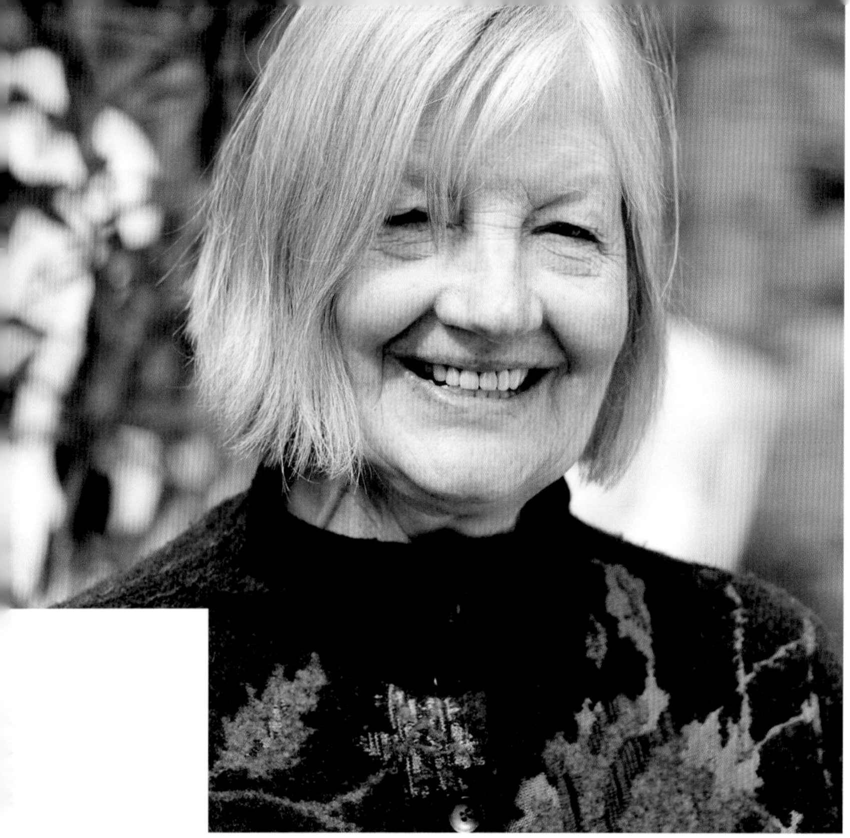

publishers, one of whom wrote back immediately and said they wanted to publish it. 'It was a very nice experience and everyone was very good to me,' she says. 'That first novel got published so easily. I got a book deal, magazines printed extracts, and then there were the various foreign rights, lunches and a Whitbread award. I thought that happened to everybody because I'd never met anyone who'd written a novel before.'

But Trapido didn't take her good fortune for granted. Her career took off just as her other friends were all re-training to be solicitors and psychoanalysts, while she got to spend her days hanging around in her pyjamas, 'lying on the floor, daydreaming and meeting people who didn't really exist.' Despite the success of her first novel, she didn't think of herself as a 'writer' for a long time. 'I just thought of it as something I did for fun.' As a result she refuses to be rushed into publishing something before she feels it is ready. 'I think I drive publishers slightly mad,' she admits. 'People say, "Unless you publish a book every two years people will forget about you," and I think, So what? I have never been ambitious, and if people forget about me, that's too bad. It's something I do for fun.'

These days, Trapido tells me, she is more professional but still very slow, and it can take a long time to move from one book to the next. 'I find once I've finished a book, I feel quite bereft at having to put those characters away, to bury them. That usually takes about a year – and of course nowadays book publishers keep you quite busy promoting the book so it's hard to get working on another.'

Trapido's books often appear complex and intricately plotted, but she denies that she plans them in detail. 'I try to feel my way to a story,' she says, eyes closed, moving her hands as if moulding a piece of clay. 'I often sit back for periods after doing this completely intuitive writing and I think, What's this book telling me about itself? And then I start to notice repeating images.' After years of working this way, she now has faith that at some point it will all connect. But sometimes, she admits, it can be like 'staring into the dark and I think, Why am I writing about these people? What have they got to do with each other, and what are they trying to say to me? And then I'll just be biking along somewhere and have little revelations, like little presents you get that drop into your mind.'

At the same time, however, Trapido is far from complacent; she works every morning from 4 to 9 AM. 'It's a better time to write because you just fall out of bed and the world's your own,' she explains. 'You can't run about visiting your friends and going shopping and all these things you do to practice work avoidance. And at four in the morning your focus is very narrow.' Once 'real life' starts and someone talks to her, though, she stops writing. 'It's sort of like "Kubla Khan,"' she says. 'Like someone walking in on your dream and breaking the magic.'

Trapido believes that, because writing creatively is 'something you do with a different part of your brain,' you need to place yourself in a different world, whether that be a quiet house at 4 AM or physically moving to another geographic location. To achieve this distance Trapido once rented a houseboat (it sank) and then bought a tiny, secluded labourer's cottage in the Oxfordshire countryside where it felt as if 'it was always four in the morning.'

There are many wonderful aspects of being a writer, but Trapido believes that one of the best is the moment you lose your inhibition. 'You can be so inhibited that you put a lock on your own mind which stops you getting it down,' she explains. 'But it actually doesn't matter if it's ghastly and embarrassing at first because no one has to see it.' Interestingly, she believes that this fear stems from childhood. 'I think the fear of embarrassing yourself by writing things down comes from being terrified as a child that someone's going to find your diary and read it.'

She finds the most difficult aspect of writing to be that she has to build a structure for herself, a problem that many writers recognise and find difficult to overcome. 'A proper job holds you together,' she says. 'You have to be respectable, wash your hair and iron your clothes, and to not do that can make you feel very disempowered. And if it's not going very well, you can think, I haven't got a proper job; I'm just hanging around wasting time.'

Trapido's final word of warning is that you should only write if you're passionate about what you're doing and believe that you're writing the best book that you possibly can. 'Don't worry about who you're directing it to, instead think about what enchants you and seduces you,' she says. 'I think if it has a magic for you and you're completely immersed in it, that will be transmitted to your readers. The magic has to completely take you over.' ■

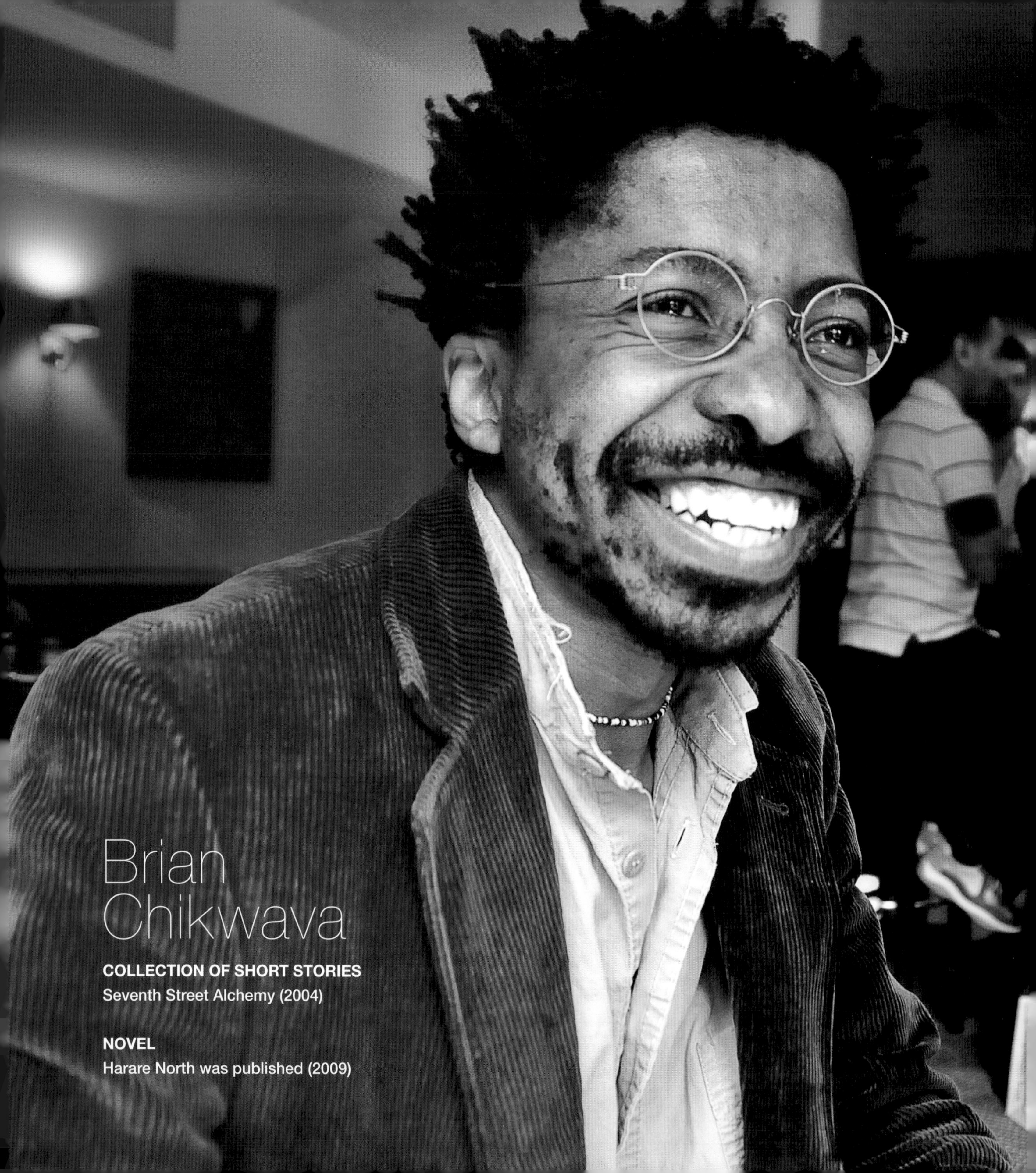

Brian Chikwava

COLLECTION OF SHORT STORIES

Seventh Street Alchemy (2004)

NOVEL

Harare North was published (2009)

In the short space of a few years, Brian Chikwava has become one of the top names among today's exciting new generation of emerging African writers. Despite an un-conventional background for a literary writer – Brian studied science at school in Harare and undertook a quantum surveying degree in the UK – he has produced award-winning work and even received a Charles Pick writing fellowship from the University of East Anglia.

In 2004, Brian Chikwava's collection of short stories *Seventh Street Alchemy* was awarded the Caine Prize (award widely known as the African Booker), making him the first Zimbabwean to receive the honour. However, there was more to this prestigious accolade than congratulations, praises and recognition. All of a sudden, Brian was under pressures of a kind he had never experienced before; agents began to court him and publishers started enquiring about a novel. 'Everyone was offering advice,' he remembers thinking 'these are empty gesture.'

In 2009, Jonathan Cape published Chikwava's first novel, *Harare North*. The title, which is a nickname for Brixton, refers to the area's large Zimbabwean population. Interestingly, despite finding an agent to support *Harare North*, the writer quickly ended the business relationship when the agent requested a synopsis. 'I did not want to scare creation away,' he explains. 'A plan gets in the way of creative mechanisms; it brings negative pressure.'

As Brian Chikwava continues to expound upon the topic of literary creation, his whole being seems to light up. 'The creative process is fragile, every time somebody knocks it off, it takes some time to start it again. When I start to write, I plug into something that only I hear so I become as open-minded as possible. That process does not fit a plan; you have to close all valves to create a vibe'. When Chikwava's creative voice manifests, he recognises it straight away. 'It can be different for each type of story', he says, 'but I can identify that little something that makes my writing. When I hit this voice, suddenly things fall into place.'

Once creativity strikes, Brian starts his work by setting the background, 'a little bit like when one moves to a new city'. Only then does he move on to developing characters. 'I need to know what to do with the environment first,' he says, 'and when that works, when I know where I am, I get the confidence to go on'. He also admits a tendency to make things more difficult for himself, 'Unwittingly I make things more difficult for myself while writing and appreciating simplicity only when I've so exhausted myself, I can hardly lift a feather.'

Despite being marketed as a specifically 'African' writer, Chikwava perceives his work differently. 'You can relate to any writing in the world as the creation of another human being,' he explains. 'As for the whole "African writer" thing, as far as I am concerned, all what it means is that an African writer will have an African sensibility, will have read African literature, anything else is a bit like putting novels in pigeonholes, it's a bit like the "plan"'.

After some more quick-fire questions, I learn that Brian's ideal superpower would be to have access to people's dreams – 'it would be a great resource for fiction,' he explains; that his biggest flop is 'trying to use longhand for initial drafts of my work'; that the books of Flann O'Brien make him both laugh and cry; and that he considers his greatest achievement to be 'mastering both Windows and Mac keyboard shortcuts.'

The author was initially wary about being interviewed for this book. He admits that he was worried about the questions and sceptical about giving advice to others. 'Every writer is very unique,' he says. 'There are things that someone can do that somebody else can't. If I take an analogy with music: when you look at a guitarist you admire, there are things you can do and some things you can't.' Ultimately, he believes that writing is a matter of confidence. 'You must not start by thinking, I can write like so and so. This is an individual journey that someone takes; you need to find the voice in your head yourself.' ■

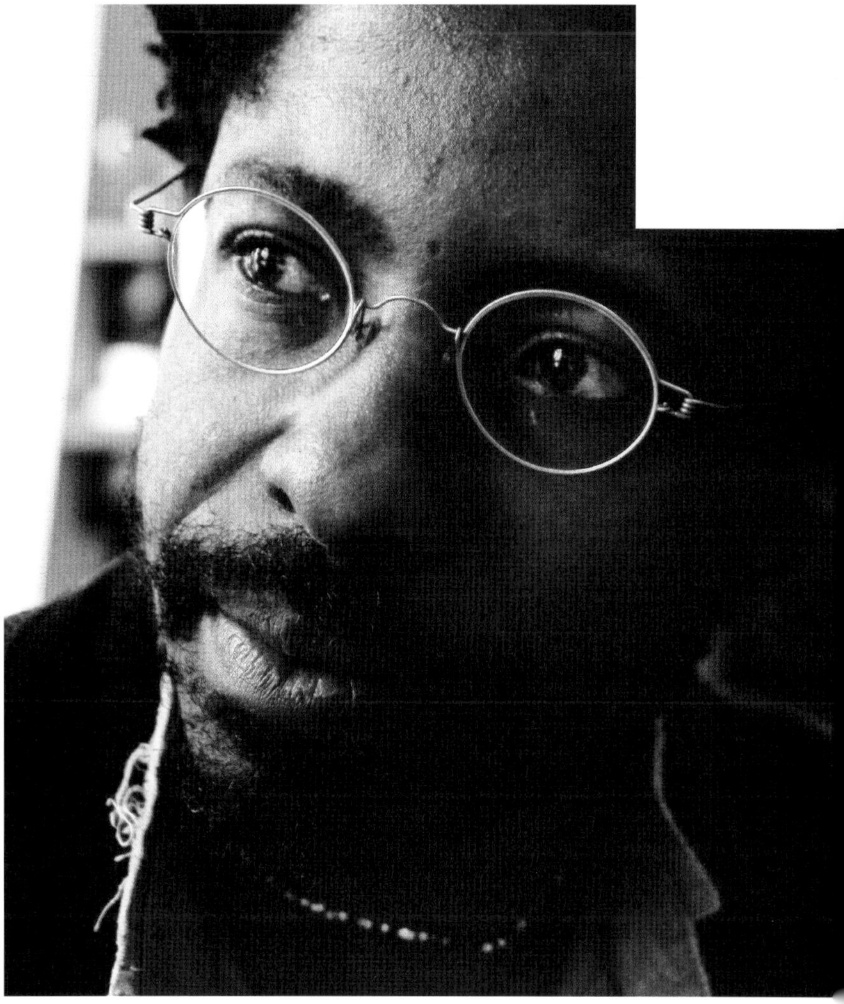

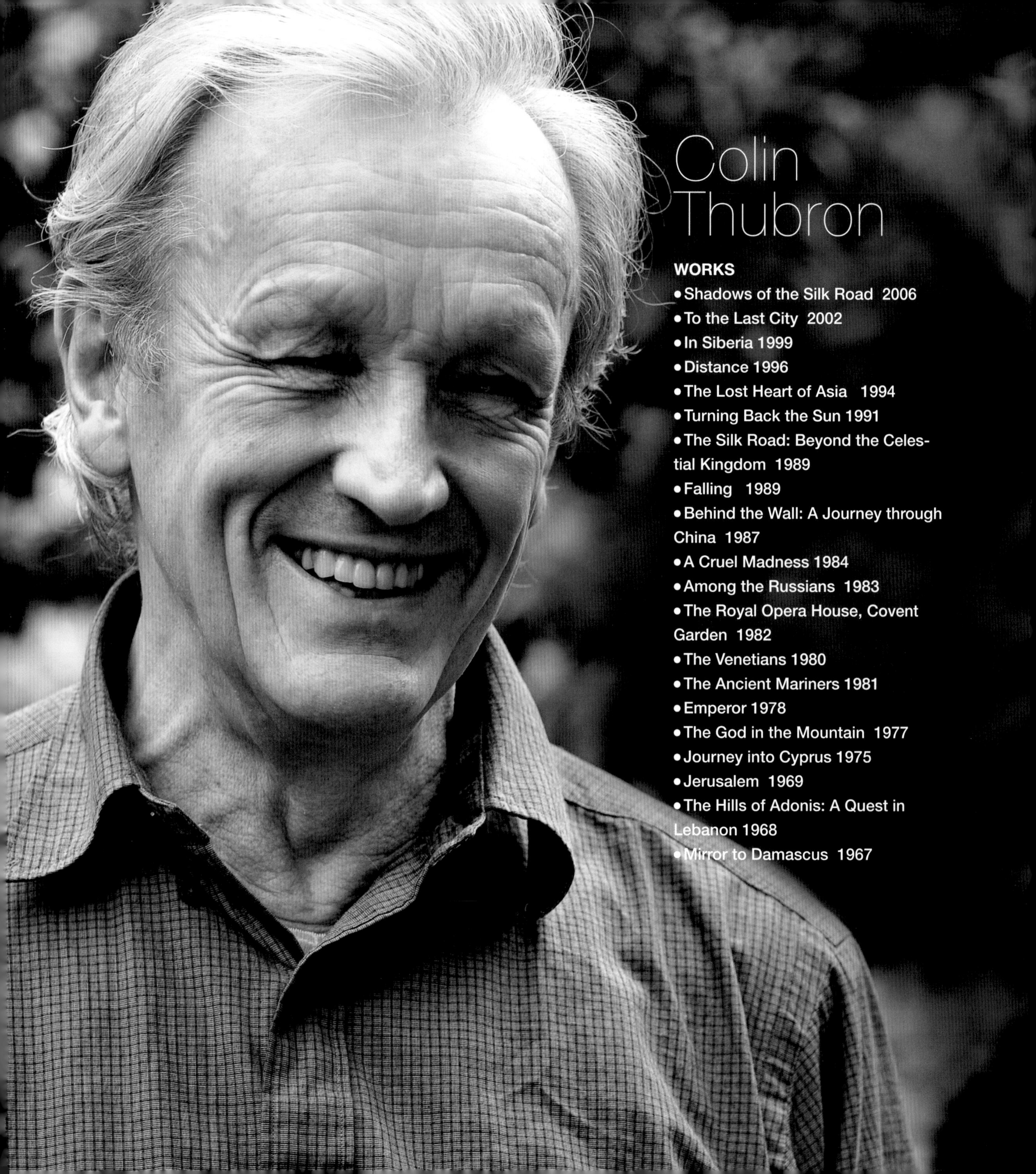

Colin Thubron

WORKS

- Shadows of the Silk Road 2006
- To the Last City 2002
- In Siberia 1999
- Distance 1996
- The Lost Heart of Asia 1994
- Turning Back the Sun 1991
- The Silk Road: Beyond the Celestial Kingdom 1989
- Falling 1989
- Behind the Wall: A Journey through China 1987
- A Cruel Madness 1984
- Among the Russians 1983
- The Royal Opera House, Covent Garden 1982
- The Venetians 1980
- The Ancient Mariners 1981
- Emperor 1978
- The God in the Mountain 1977
- Journey into Cyprus 1975
- Jerusalem 1969
- The Hills of Adonis: A Quest in Lebanon 1968
- Mirror to Damascus 1967

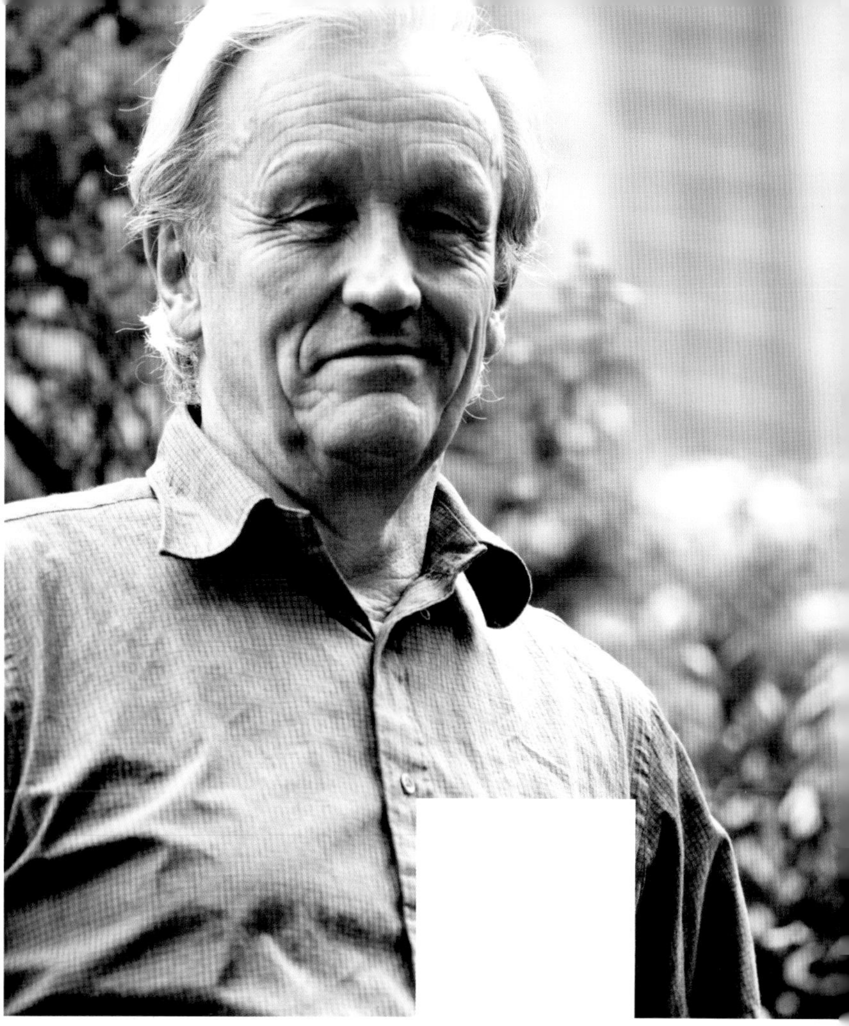

When award-winning travel writer Colin Thubron published his first travelogue, Mirror to Damascus, in 1967, he introduced readers to a land seldom associated with casual journeys. These days, Thubron – who lives in London – is a revered elder of travel writing, with books that rank among the travel classics.

For some, travel writing seems like the Holy Grail of jobs: difficult to get but easy to do. After all, most of us have travelled at some point in life. However, the author informs me that travel writing is nowhere near as simple as it appears.

'Travel writing,' he explains, 'requires you to have contradictory qualities: you have to be tough and hardy to do the travelling, but you need to be sensitive to write. Therefore, an awful lot of books are published by people who are not very adventurous travellers but are very good writers, or the opposite; they do something very hardy, difficult and dashing but can't write about it. It is a hard genre that requires a lot of you - more than any other genre I can think of.'

Essentially, one needs to have a good journey to write a good book. Colin Thubron always strives to do 'extra things to make the words good and interesting.' When I remark that this could be pushed too far, he nods sagely. 'As a writer, you are so fascinated by looking out that you forget that you yourself are vulnerable, so you do things you would never normally dare to do. I can really understand how war photographers get shot, because they see the world through that rectangle of the camera and don't believe they are there.'

On the day of our interview, Thubron has just completed a trip. Despite having returned to the UK in the early hours of the morning, he appears fresh and composed. I can't help wondering where he gets his energy from. 'I find that because I take a journey, in order to turn it into a book, I am less afraid, bored, or tired.' This solo globe-trotter then throws a truly novel idea my way.

'There are two of you travelling,' he says, smiling fleetingly at my obvious surprise. 'There is the one making the journey and having a difficult time. Then there is the other one seated on his shoulder, writing. So, even if the writer is having a really tough time, such as being beaten up or shot, it is good copy. At least you can say that it is part of the personality of the country. You need to do these things to get another kind of data. It gives you something extra, a frisson.'

What sort of problems do travel writers encounter? Unlike most writers, Colin Thubron has never had a manuscript rejected. However, he says that one problem with travel writing is that a journey from A to B is just not enough. 'You need a thread, and that's the hardest thing to find.' His preferred method of finding this 'thread' is through research. What he's looking for, he says, is a feeling of 'Ah! That is what this country means.'

There is also the problem of recording. Like many famous travellers before him, he writes his impressions, conversations and observations in little notebooks. At the end of a trip, he ends up carrying with him a serious bundle of these precious little booklets, which can sometimes spell disaster. For instance, he recalls that during his first journey to Russia, 'I almost had my notebooks confiscated by the KGB, but I managed to get them back.' During work on his last book, he emailed his notes to himself whenever he could to avoid similar situations.

In addition to these possible setbacks, gaining access to individuals or areas can be challenging – and not just because of the authorities. 'You have to get through many barriers to have proper access to people,' Colin says, ' such as the barriers of politics and politeness, and these are not to be ignored in Asia.' The travel writer also has to beware of fatigue. He explains, 'You are seeking knowledge and understanding: not just intellectual understanding of a society or a culture, but a sort of sensuous, emotional experience or understanding, which means that you have to immerse yourself, and that can be very demanding.'

However, he leaves me with a final encouraging word of advice. 'Travel writing is very demanding, but if it is not demanding you are probably not doing it well. And have fun too – that's very important.'

Colin has just completed a trip to Tibet. We can look forward to his intelligent portrayal of a country much talked about but about which very little is known. ■

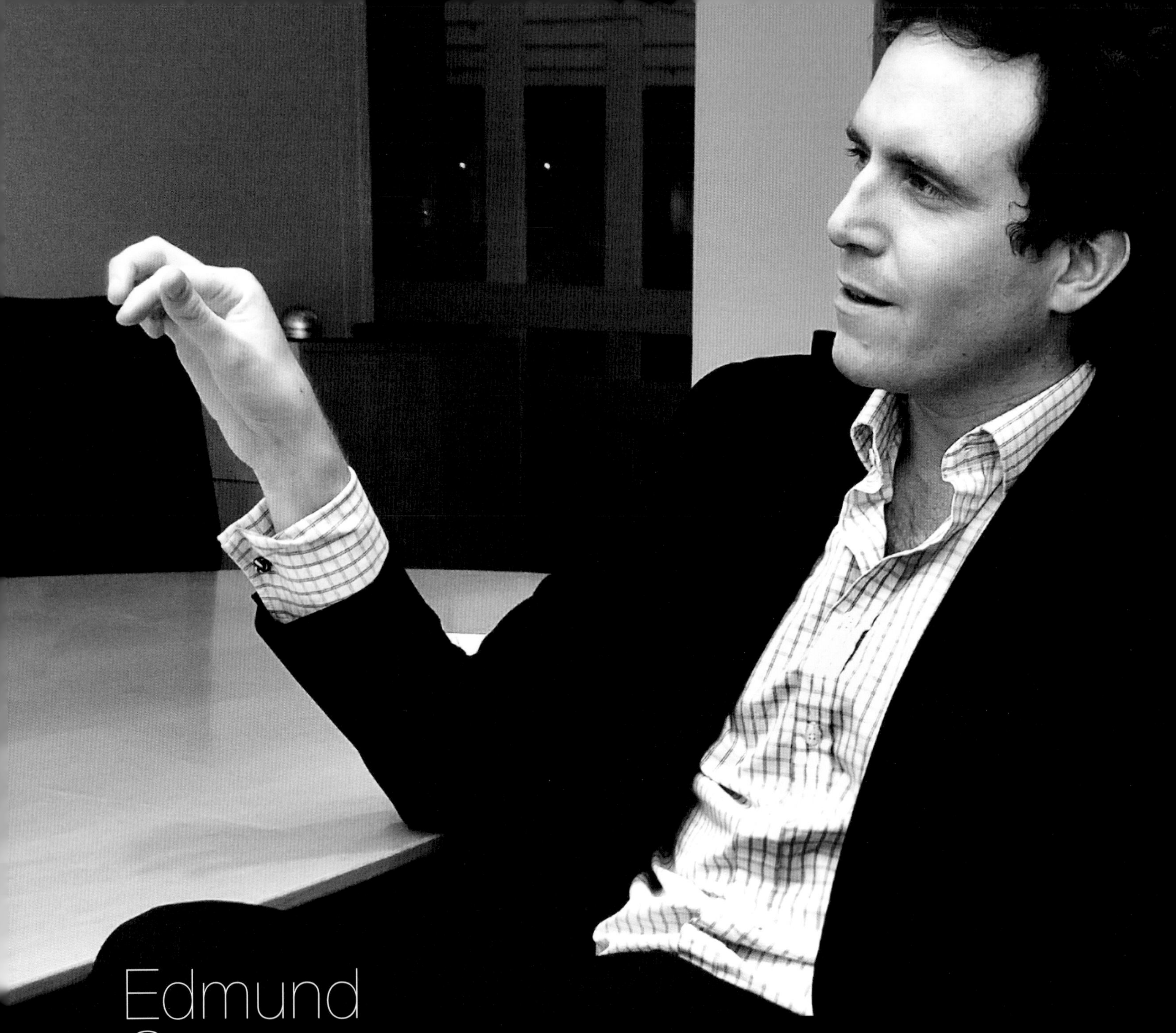

Edmund Conway

Edmund Conway is the economics editor of the Daily Telegraph and author of 50 Economic Ideas You Really Need to Know (2009).

Edmund Conway never had any particular interest in economics. In his youth he was 'obsessed' with writing and spent his days writing comic book adventures and political plays, as well as dabbling in music and art. Odd, then, that at the age of 25 he became economics editor at the Daily Telegraph and wrote his first book on the subject before he hit 30.

He describes the circumstances leading up to his career as 'all just luck, a lot of luck. You fall into things by accident, and that's basically what happened with me.' He volunteered to stuff envelopes at the Telegraph when he was sixteen, went on to join the newspaper's trainee scheme after leaving university and, although he was 'desperate' not to end up on the City desk, that's exactly where he found himself. 'I had no economics qualifications,' Conway says, 'and I'm pretty poor at maths. I was just working it out as I went along, working from textbooks and talking to people and asking stupid questions.'

In retrospect, he realises that it was this period of his life that inspired him to write *50 Economic Ideas You Really Need to Know*. 'When I started writing about economics, there was no comprehensive book I could turn to – nothing to tell me how on earth interest rates work or why globalisation is such a big deal.' At first, he admits, he was totally overwhelmed, but quickly realised that it was 'immensely simple' once he deciphered the jargon surrounding the subject.

After a few years as an economics reporter and a brief stint as the Daily Mail's very first economics correspondent, Conway returned to the Telegraph as economics editor. 'I was in the right place at the right time and so I ended up at the age of 25, almost 26, with this title of economics editor, which was incredibly terrifying,' he laughs. It was then that he began to seriously consider writing a book that explained economics in simple terms. 'My skill, if I have one, is explaining things to people, making them seem accessible and hopefully interesting,' he says. 'I'd always hoped to put that into a book and then I heard that Quercus were looking for someone to write something similar.' He shrugs. 'It seemed fortuitously to fit in with the kind of book I had been wanting to write. I was really lucky. I've been really lucky each step of the way.'

The financial crisis was the next lucky thing for Conway, because although it was the busiest period of his professional life, it sparked an interest in economics among the general public. Suddenly everyone wanted to know how economics affected them. However, it also made the writing process quite stressful. 'We had quite a short lead time,' he recalls. 'I think I started writing in August 2008 and delivery was supposed to be at the end of that same year.' Conway wrote mainly on weekends and days off, only taking one week off work to 'break the back' of the book, cutting himself off from all distraction by retreating to a friend's chalet in the Alps – though this caused him to miss the collapse of Lehman Brothers and the bailout of HBOS, which he describes as 'the most dramatic period of the global financial system ever.'

Conway remembers, with some horror, finishing a frantic day at the paper and going straight to Maida Vale Library to work on his book. 'I do a 9-to-5 job that can be quite stressful. I usually get home and do something creative like DJing because it's completely different from what I do during the day, but doing the book didn't feel like that.' He wonders if it's different for fiction writers, for whom writing is an escape. 'I was writing about economics and so I was bringing the office home in a way that you don't usually do in journalism.'

Another aspect of writing Conway finds stressful is the editing process. 'It was quite tough to jump back into a chapter and rethink it entirely; it almost takes more energy than writing it in the first place.' But what really surprised him was that once it was published, he had to do all the publicity himself – quite a significant task for a first-time author. 'I only learned this after I spoke to an agent friend of mine,' Conway recalls. 'He advised me to set aside a certain portion of my advance for publicity, because the chances are you'll have to put in all the legwork yourself, particularly these days.' Fortunately, as Conway worked for a national newspaper, he managed to persuade his editor to serialise the book. 'The publicity thing is really important because there's a lot of extra work you have to do,' he warns. ▶

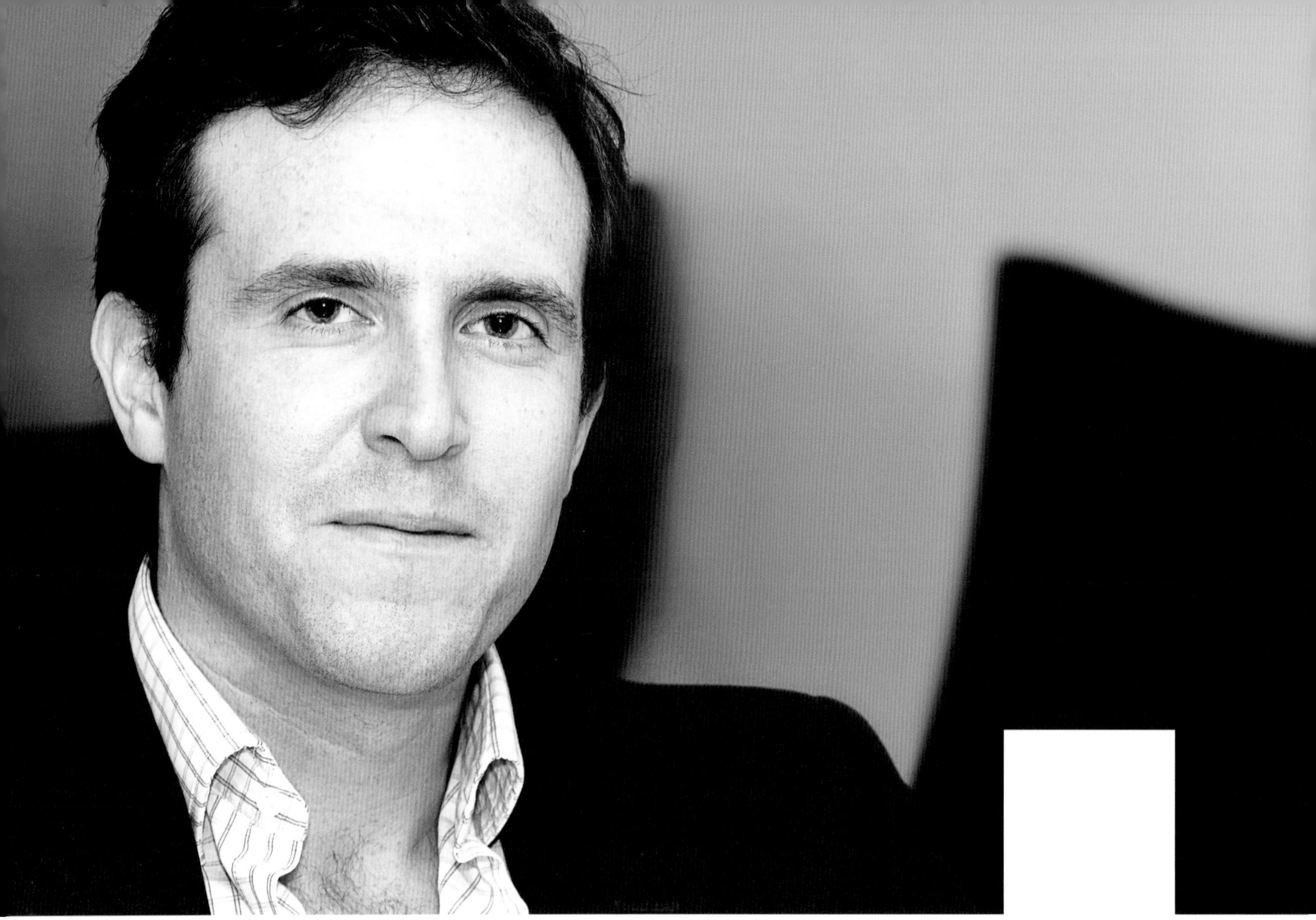

'I hadn't expected it at all. But don't take it personally - it's a normal experience for most authors. It's a struggling industry and as a result they don't have that many resources.'

I ask him what one piece of advice he would give aspiring authors. He pauses for a few moments. 'Don't be offended by rejection because you've got to put up with a lot quite early on,' he says. 'I think it's one of the most, if not the most, difficult occupations out there because it involves such a degree of self-sufficiency and personal determination and such long periods of not having anyone validate you.' He pauses again. 'But it's so massively rewarding when you finally get to see your name in print.'

Despite all his hard work (or perhaps because of it), Conway hasn't yet read his book in printed form. 'I have occasionally had to refer to it, though. I've got a copy of it by my desk and sometimes when it comes to something like the GDP figures, I go back to it and think, Wow, I used to know that?' ■

Find out more at www.edmundconway.com

Dr. Anna Whitelock

- Bedfellows (upcoming release)
- Mary Tudor: England's First Queen (2009)

Although history books and historical fiction fulfil different functions, historians and novelists can be equally inspiring. Some histories fascinate, some books act like a stepping stone to learn more about a subject. Dr. Anna Whitelock's début *Mary Tudor: England's First Queen*, an absorbing biography of Queen Mary the first, is a prime example of such writing.

When I meet up with Dr. Whitelock at Royal Holloway, University of London, where she teaches early modern history, I immediately notice her office's wall-to-wall bookshelves. I begin by asking about her decision to popularise her academic knowledge and her take on the distinctness of historical biographies. Settling in her computer chair, she tells me, 'It is a real challenge to write history in the way that the public wants to read, but I wanted to try. I was conscious of the fact that a lot of academic work is not made available to a wider audience, and I think that it should be.'

I ask Anna what she thinks the differences are between factual history writing and historical fiction?

'Historical novelists try to inhabit the body of the character and explore the emotional terrain in a way that if you rely on cold hard evidence, you can't do. It is like filling in the gaps of where the record takes us but at the same time being true to the record.'

Whitelock's own PhD focused on the court of Mary I. Today's literary market already contains a wide range – some would say an excess - of books on the Tudor dynasty. However, when it comes to Mary Tudor, the average person on the street is unlikely to know much beyond the 'Bloody Mary' quasi-legend. 'My Mary story,' says Dr. Whitelock, 'was as compelling as that of Elizabeth, and I wanted it to have that kind of exposure. I wanted to tell the story to a much wider range of people, to disseminate academic work to a wider audience.'

Achieving this goal was a fairly obstacle-free process for Whitelock. From the outset, she had a strong sense of what she wanted her book to be. 'I was writing the book I wanted to read, that was my guiding principle.' Through a friend, she found an agent who turned out to be 'a good guiding presence.' She also managed to structure her writing schedule around her day job. 'I was busy teaching during the day and wrote in the evenings,' she recalls. 'I wrote a very detailed proposal with a summary of the chapters, a few expanded chapters and a basic picture of the target market as I saw it.'

Her proposal was met with interest from seven publishers. 'There was an auction for the book,' she tells me. 'Two publishing houses - Bloomsbury and Viking- made similar offers, so the choice came down to other factors such as the editor.' With her agent's guidance, Anna ultimately chose Bloomsbury.

Through her insightful research, Dr. Whitelock had come to appreciate Mary as 'a courageous and very troubled figure; a determined one too, but with a determination born out of adversity.' As

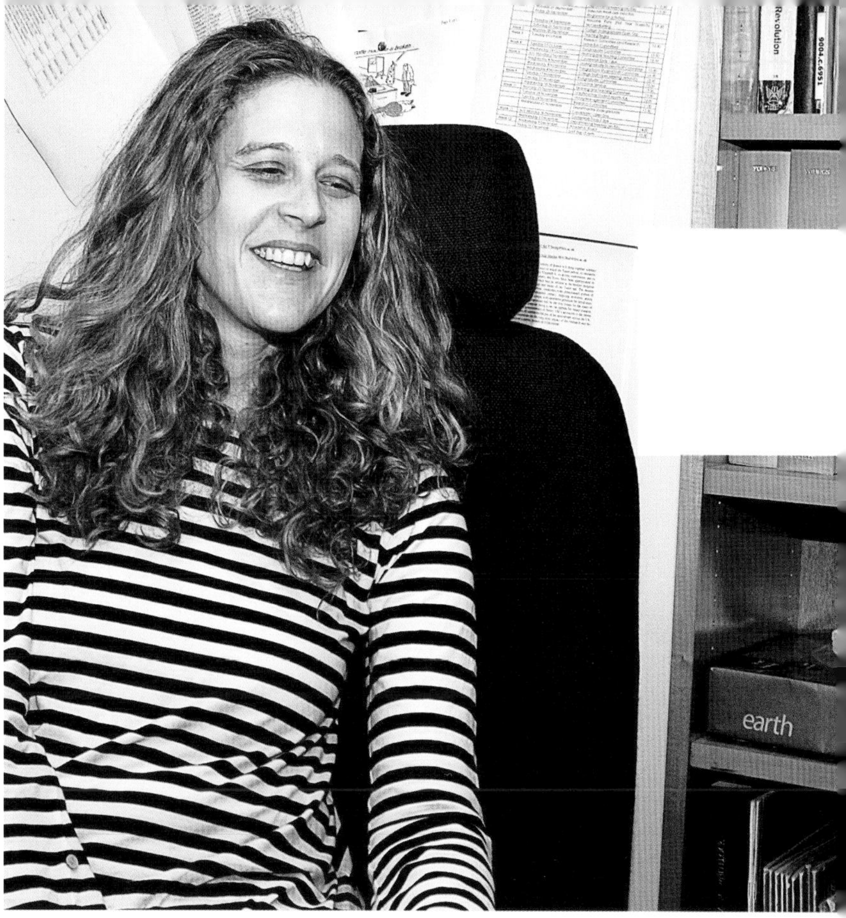

she talks about her specialist subject, her enthusiasm rises visibly. 'I was not trying to write an apologetic account of Mary's life, but I was trying to understand what was going on. The whole idea of Bloody Mary comes from John Foxe's Book of Martyrs and Mary became a caricature developed by the Elizabethans, so I was peeling off the layers of propaganda.'

As Anna was already in possession of the bulk of the research and backed up by a solid synopsis, writing the book should have been straightforward. Writing for a new, non-academic market, however, meant adapting her material and approach to different readers' needs. 'My editor, who has a sense of the market and people who were going to read it, was coming in with big broad-brush ideas to make the book bolder, more European, bigger and more outward-looking, and that informed the writing process. For instance, I included a good deal about Mary's Spanish heritage in the book.'

Since completing Mary Tudor: England's First Queen, Anna has had time to reflect on the difficulties writers need to deal with. 'It is a long slog,' she explains. 'You have to be able to manage time and keep the adrenalin pumping. It is easy when there are meetings with the publisher or the editor, but otherwise you spend weeks and months writing. The whole idea that there is a book at the end of it becomes more and more distant, but people are waiting for it, so you have to try to maintain a sense of urgency. It is stressful and the pressure can be paralysing.' ■

www.annawhitelock.co.uk

Esther Freud

NOVELS

- Love Falls (2007)
- The Sea House (2003)
- The Wild (2000)
- Gaglow (1997)
- Peerless Flats (1993)
- Hideous Kinky (1992)

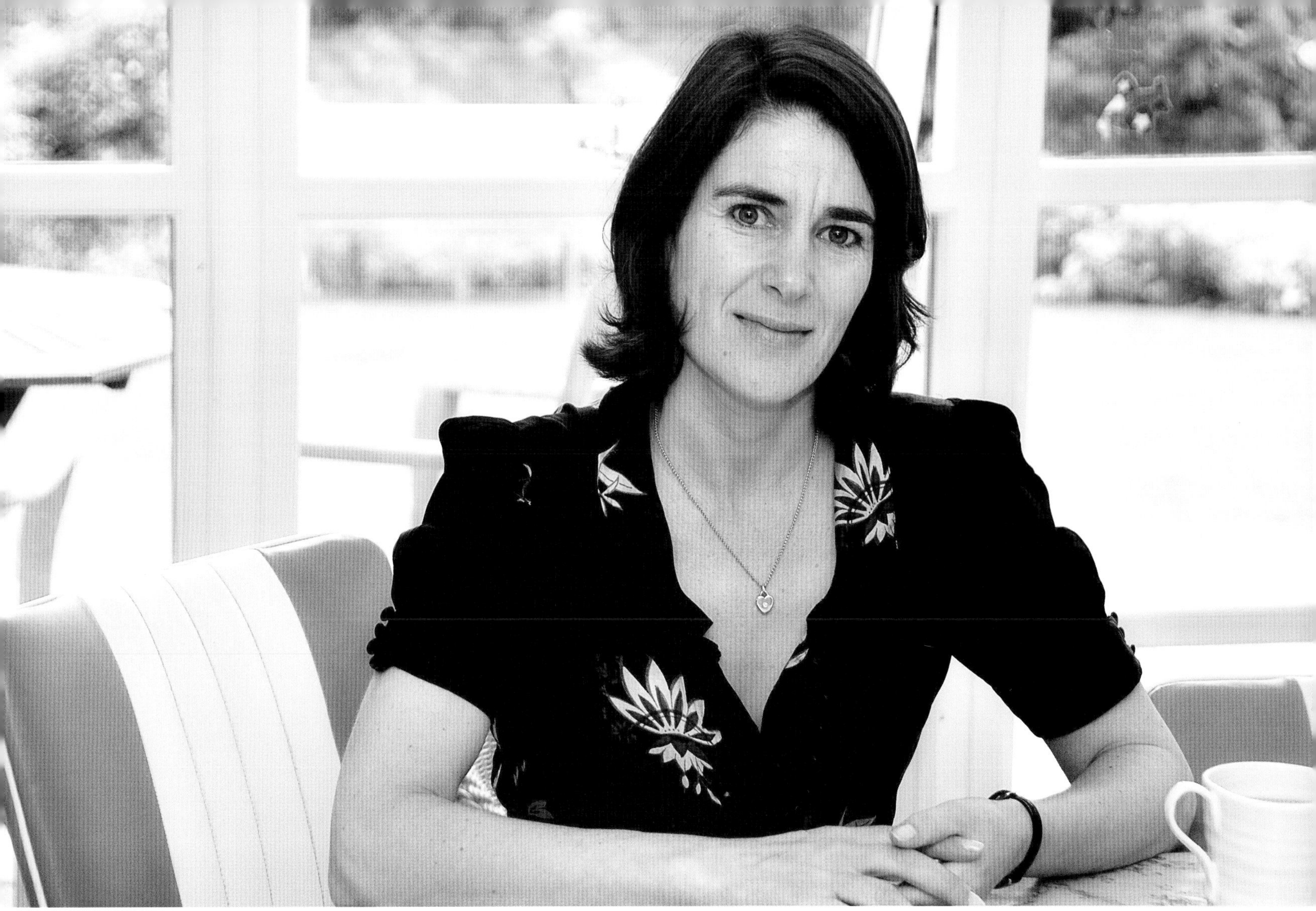

As a child, Esther Freud was always making things - sewing, knitting or moulding sculptures out of clay. She believes this need to create led her through a career as an actress to emerge as an author.

'I loved stories, but I didn't imagine I would be a writer,' she says. Despite never watching television in her youth (her father, the painter Lucian Freud, and her mother sent her to a Steiner school) and rarely going to the theatre, she quickly decided she wanted to be an actress. 'I wanted to tell stories, but I wanted to physically embody what I did more than writing involves.'

Even from an early age, Freud knew that she wanted to leave school after sixteen and have a life that didn't revolve around writing essays. 'I felt I saw through it,' she explains. 'I saw that they were telling me something and I had to re-organise it in a clever way and tell it back. I just didn't see the point and I didn't want to do it for one second longer than I had to, so I began to make plans for how to avoid all that.'

Not surprisingly, she did indeed leave school at sixteen to enrol in drama school. 'It was wonderful,' she recalls. 'But I was frustrated with the fact that so much of the time you weren't able to be creative – that was the truth. So much of the time you were just waiting.' After leaving drama school and finding herself in between jobs, Freud started to write and found it enjoyable precisely because she didn't have to do it - and after embarking upon a creative writing course, she developed a passion for it. 'I really loved it,' she says. 'I really felt I was getting at certain strange memories and I learnt to express myself on the page in a way that I never thought possible.'

For a period she found the perfect combination of writing and performing, penning shows with a fellow actress. 'I just felt completely happy,' Freud says. 'I was doing exactly what I wanted to be doing. I personally would have been happy to go on writing like that forever; I had no desire to sit down and write on my own and impose the ▶

discipline on myself that it takes to write a novel.' However, her friend disappeared to do a film and Freud, bereft of her creative partner and becoming dissatisfied with her own career, continued to jot down notes for what would become her first novel.

Despite having no idea of how to put her flashbacks and episodes into a structure, Freud continued writing in between acting jobs until she had a revelation. 'One day, after an acting job had come to an end, I just had this real feeling of "Oh my God, I'm just starting again, all the time," which is what acting is.'

The following day, she decided to sit down for three hours to work on her book (although, she tells me, it felt too presumptuous to call it that at the time) and write every day until she got another job. 'I was completely in love with the process,' she says. 'And when I eventually finished my first novel and it was accepted, I got this extraordinary

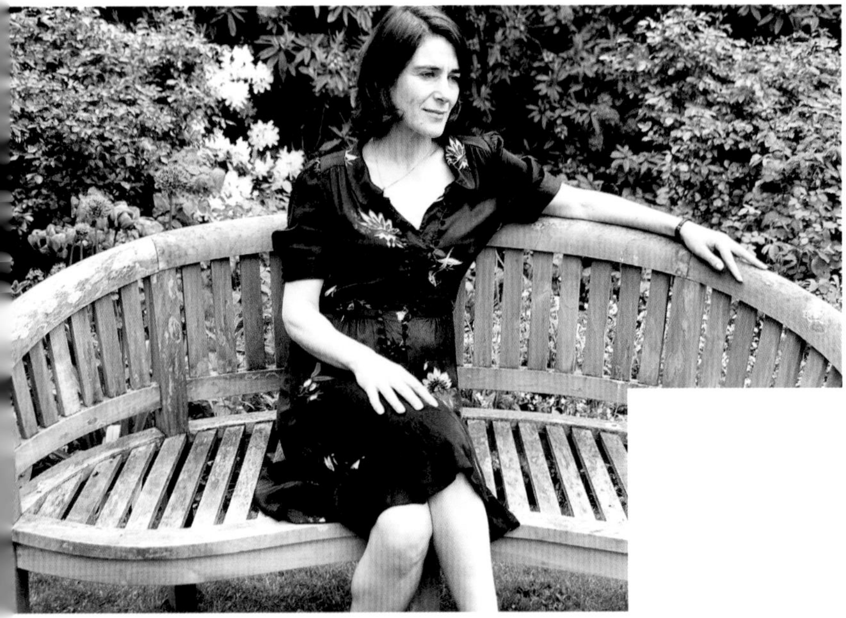

boost of confidence that I'd never had as an actress. The confidence given by someone saying, "We love what you've already done," and for it then to be made permanent, was a very different experience. I very, very quickly wrote my second novel, just out of the sheer exuberant feeling I got when the first was accepted. I had this amazing feeling of energy and I have just carried on ever since.'

For Freud, writing fulfilled a creative yearning that acting never did. 'I started to write and found that in a strange way you were making something,' she explains. 'Even though you were just writing, you were making whole worlds; you were making all these characters come to life. You were taking someone on a journey and I loved that, and from then on I was pretty much addicted.'

Of course, there are still difficulties. The words don't always flow as easily as they did with that second book. 'Like anyone, I've had times when what I'm trying to do doesn't seem to work,' she admits. 'And that's hard. There are times when I feel I can't get into this again; I just don't think I can. It's like twisting a huge piece of metal into a different shape: you think you just don't have the strength, but then you find you do, especially if you do it bit by bit.'

Writers have myriad ways of tackling what some call 'writer's block' – many have to temporarily abandon what they're doing and look at it later with fresh eyes, but Freud handles the problem differently. 'For me it's always better just to write,' she reveals. 'I'm not very good at thinking without writing, so when I start writing that's when it starts to come out.'

Freud finds she has an energy in the mornings that seems to be specially reserved for writing. 'I'm quite careful with that energy. I need to channel it,' she says. 'Writing recharges me. I feel peaceful and not exhausted if I've done my three or four hours in the morning. It really works for me and it doesn't matter where I am, as long as I write in the morning.' But she has to balance this with her home life (she is married to the actor David Morrissey, with whom she has three children), which can sometimes be tricky. 'I sometimes feel very out of sync with my family,' she says. 'They've been out all day and they want to relax at home, whereas I've been alone at home all day and I just want to go out. I have to sometimes go out just before they come back so that I'm in the same space as them, otherwise there's this sort of restlessness about me that they don't have and it creates a disharmony.'

Interestingly, she is one of the few authors who admit that a review has influenced their writing. Freud doesn't usually attach much significance to reviews, although occasionally, if she hasn't got that one review that really understood her book, she is left with a 'slight hankering' for someone to 'give back' what she felt she gave out. However, one negative review actually caused her to 'up her game,' and in hindsight she credits the reviewer with making her a better writer. 'He accused me of being a bit lazy and a bit repetitive,' she tells me. 'I was very taken aback that he was so unimpressed by the autobiographical content of my work - God, it was only my second book – but he really hit his mark and I decided to do something much more imaginative and much less autobiographical. It was a huge challenge, but it was really exciting and it led me in a really interesting direction, so I'm grateful.'

Freud hasn't had to deal with too much rejection during her literary career, but she finds that any rejection and criticism that does come her way is pretty easy to take after being an actress. 'It definitely makes you thicker-skinned,' she states. 'You often hear writers complain of what a hard life it is and I just say, "Try acting - you just have no idea." Writing is such a privileged life because you're in control of your own creativity and you can have a fantastic day and no one has to tell you that you can. To me that's the ultimate luxury. I might sigh with weariness or loneliness occasionally, but even twenty years on, I appreciate it so much.' ■

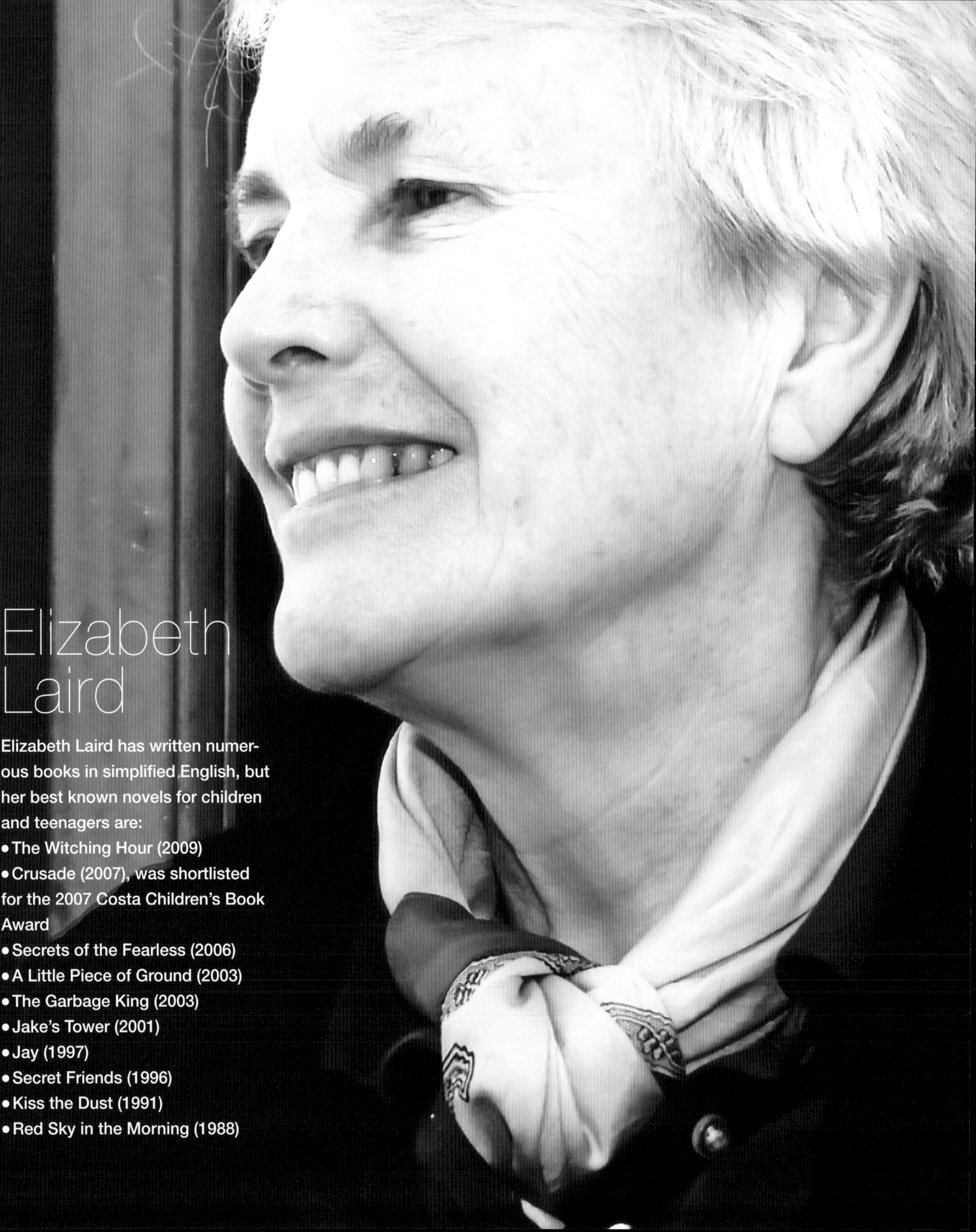

Elizabeth Laird

Elizabeth Laird has written numerous books in simplified English, but her best known novels for children and teenagers are:

- The Witching Hour (2009)
- Crusade (2007), was shortlisted for the 2007 Costa Children's Book Award
- Secrets of the Fearless (2006)
- A Little Piece of Ground (2003)
- The Garbage King (2003)
- Jake's Tower (2001)
- Jay (1997)
- Secret Friends (1996)
- Kiss the Dust (1991)
- Red Sky in the Morning (1988)

As the author of nearly 150 books, which have been translated into fifteen foreign languages, Elizabeth Laird is the voice of experience when it comes to writing for young readers.

'As children's writers we are both lucky and unlucky. We don't get any space in the newspaper because there are very few reviews, JK Rowling has made a real difference; she was so spectacularly popular that now lots of people think they can write children's books.'

'When children's books are popular they can be in print for years, because they are used in school. One of my books has been in print since 1988. The girls who read it when they were twelve are now buying it for their own children. If you can get into the curriculum, you have a small but solid base which lasts longer than that of novels for adults.'

In contrast to most writers, who have to send their first book to countless publishers and receive rejection after rejection, Elizabeth Laird had somebody waiting for her.

'This is where children's books are different from other books. When I was teaching English in Ethiopia, I wrote some stories in simplified English for my students, and when I came back to England, there were educational publishers who wanted to publish books like that. They came round to educational establishments and asked us to try to do that kind of thing. I got four or five books published from that.'

'When I had my own children, I used to analyse what they liked and I wrote my own stories on what I thought little children liked, so I wrote little picture books. I had to go to several publishers before these got published but eventually they were accepted. Then when I got an editor, one day she said, "I think it's about time you wrote a novel", so I had somebody waiting for me. I came into it slowly and built confidence slowly.'

As we move on to the subject of inspiration, Laird reveals the origins of her stories. 'Most authors copy other authors,' she says. 'They want to write another Harry Potter or Agatha Christie. They don't look deeply enough into themselves. Usually, I start with a strong feeling, which then leads into a story. It might be jealousy, it might be anger, or courage, or the power of love.'

'Then I build the characters up and flesh things out from there. Everything comes from the characters. They have got to be real people; you have to care if they live or die. If you don't care about them, the readers will not care either.'

'When I wrote *The Garbage King*, which is set among street children in Ethiopia, what attracted me to the idea was the loneliness of it and that sense of camaraderie. When the West invaded Iraq, I was so angry, I decided to write a novel about the Crusades. I thought, 'They have done it before and it did not work then; it was not a good idea then and it is not a good idea now'.'

Most authors have some sort of writing routine, and Elizabeth Laird is no exception. 'I am not somebody who has written a best-seller and can live on that,' she says. 'I need the money. This is my job. My husband is a writer too, so we have created a way of life whereby writing is our routine. I start writing in the morning between 8:00 and 9:00 and stop when I am exhausted.'

'I don't go to events very often now-a-days. I have a website which really is for children and schools. They can click on a book and talk about it, or they can write me letters, which I answer.'

I soon learn that Elizabeth Laird considers authors, especially children's authors, to have a special responsibility to readers. 'What do authors do? We help people to step into somebody else's shoes and walk around in them for a while. That teaches empathy - readers become that person,' she explains. 'Then that expands our understanding of human beings, which makes us more open to tolerance, understanding, kindness. This is one reason why children's writers have to be much more responsible about what they write than other authors. We want to entertain children, but we also want them to grow.'

I ask Elizabeth if she has any advice for new writers. 'My first novel, *Red Sky in the Morning*, is about my own childhood and my own younger brother. I think it is a good idea to start by examining a personal experience and then turning it into fiction. Writing a first novel is very daunting, and it helps to dig into your own background.'

She also encourages aspiring authors not to give up. 'A lot of people who want to be writers don't want to do the writing. A lot of people don't realise how difficult it is to get published and make a living. You always feel that you can do better and you always feel every book is something new and potentially wonderful. You always feel like that, every time. And sometimes it is something different and wonderful, and sometimes it is actually much worse than what you have done before. You have to keep experimenting.'

'I always advise to read and practice writing as much as you can,' concludes Laird, 'but to also open yourself to other experiences and people. Be aware of what is going on around you, and then ponder what you have done and seen and heard - that is how you start.' ■

To learn more about Elizabeth Laird and her work, visit: http://www.elizabethlaird.co.uk/

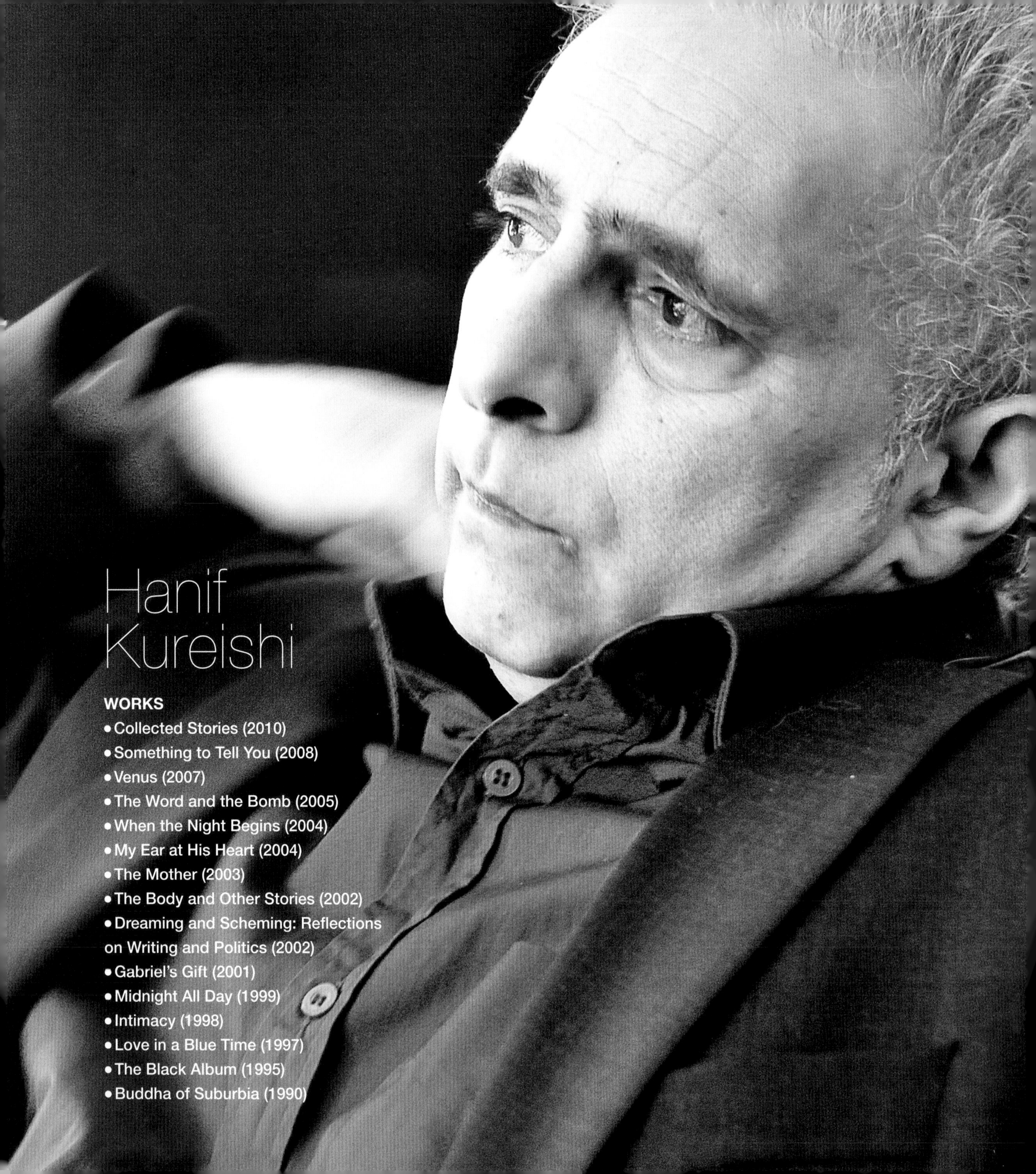

Hanif Kureishi

WORKS

- Collected Stories (2010)
- Something to Tell You (2008)
- Venus (2007)
- The Word and the Bomb (2005)
- When the Night Begins (2004)
- My Ear at His Heart (2004)
- The Mother (2003)
- The Body and Other Stories (2002)
- Dreaming and Scheming: Reflections on Writing and Politics (2002)
- Gabriel's Gift (2001)
- Midnight All Day (1999)
- Intimacy (1998)
- Love in a Blue Time (1997)
- The Black Album (1995)
- Buddha of Suburbia (1990)

Hanif Kureishi decided that he wanted to be a writer at the age of fifteen and from that moment he set about rigorously pursuing that goal. Coming from a family of writers, he also recognised the skills he needed to become a writer.

Prolificacy and a thick hide were the main attributes he considered – and still considers – essential to a successful writing career. 'The amount is important. I can't emphasise that enough,' he says. 'I wrote two or three novels after school and I can see now that it was very good training in terms of constructing a whole book. I learned a lot by writing a lot; that's how you do it. Now I teach writing and, in my view, my students don't write enough.'

Although none of these early attempts were published, they did catch the eye of the editor Jeremy Trafford, who quickly became a friend and mentor. 'He used to come to my house,' Kureishi says. 'He taught me and helped me a lot with my writing. My father was also a writing teacher, and I've learned a lot from directors and editors that I've worked with. I've had a lot of teachers.'

Kureishi does not seem to suffer from the lack of self-confidence that blights many writers and prevents them from showing their work to others. 'It is difficult to open yourself up to criticism,' he admits. 'But you have to put up with it - otherwise it's worse when you get a bad review. People get too hung up on quality control. They should just write any rubbish. If you get too hung up on it, too self-conscious, you'll just stop.'

Initially, Kureishi found his feet as a playwright and screenwriter in the dusty wings of The Royal Court Theatre. 'If you're young and you're smart, you find people smarter than you to teach you,' he says. 'I went to university, but The Royal Court was really my university. There were some very intelligent people there.' Was it this training that left Kureishi more open to a collaborative, often painful, approach to writing? 'The collaborative element partly stemmed from working in the theatre,' he concurs. 'But mainly it was just being smart enough to realise you need intelligent comment.' Physical evidence of this can be found on the original manuscript of The Buddha of Suburbia, which bears the marks and scrawls of Kureishi's American editor, British editor and his then-girlfriend Tracy, as well as his own.

Despite his many successes in the theatre and on screen, Kureishi yearned to write a novel – and all it took for that to happen was being nominated for an Oscar. The success of his film *My Beautiful Laundrette* enabled Kureishi to disengage himself from the world of film and focus on writing novels. 'I had some money, so I could buy two years, and I wrote *The Buddha of Suburbia* during that time,' he explains. 'That was the book that I had been working up to writing; that was the one. I had the material, I had the passion and at that age I finally had enough craft to write it.'

Even with his Oscar nominations and literary awards, Kureishi still finds the life of a writer difficult. 'It's very, very difficult to make a living all your life out of writing,' he says. 'It's a really hard thing to do. I wouldn't recommend it. Some years you make very little. In the 1980s I was on the dole and lived in a council flat. I didn't really make any serious money for about ten years after that.' Now that Kureishi teaches and writes novels as well as films, he describes his career as 'a hustle.'

In his early days, occasional dips in his self-belief and finances gave the normally cocksure Kureishi reason to doubt whether writing was really for him. 'I kept going because it's my job,' he explains. 'I like it and I'm very obsessive about it, and I couldn't give up because I always thought that I had something to say and that other people didn't, but it's a real struggle; it's a struggle with yourself.' And the bad news is that he believes it is now harder than ever for writers to break into the industry.

'The publishing industry has become consolidated,' he tells me. 'Publishers were small, but now they're basically big corporations and they're getting bigger, which means it's very hard to get through. And it's going to be much more difficult now,' he adds. 'The amount of books published is really going to decline because of the economic situation.'

There are, however, a few bright spots in this otherwise gloomy forecast. Apple's iPad is set to be released the day after our interview, which Kureishi believes will change the way we read books forever. 'Ebooks are going to work,' he says. 'People are going to be downloading ebooks like they never have before; tomorrow the revolution starts.' This positive attitude does not stretch to self-publishing, though. 'Self-publishing is pretty ▶

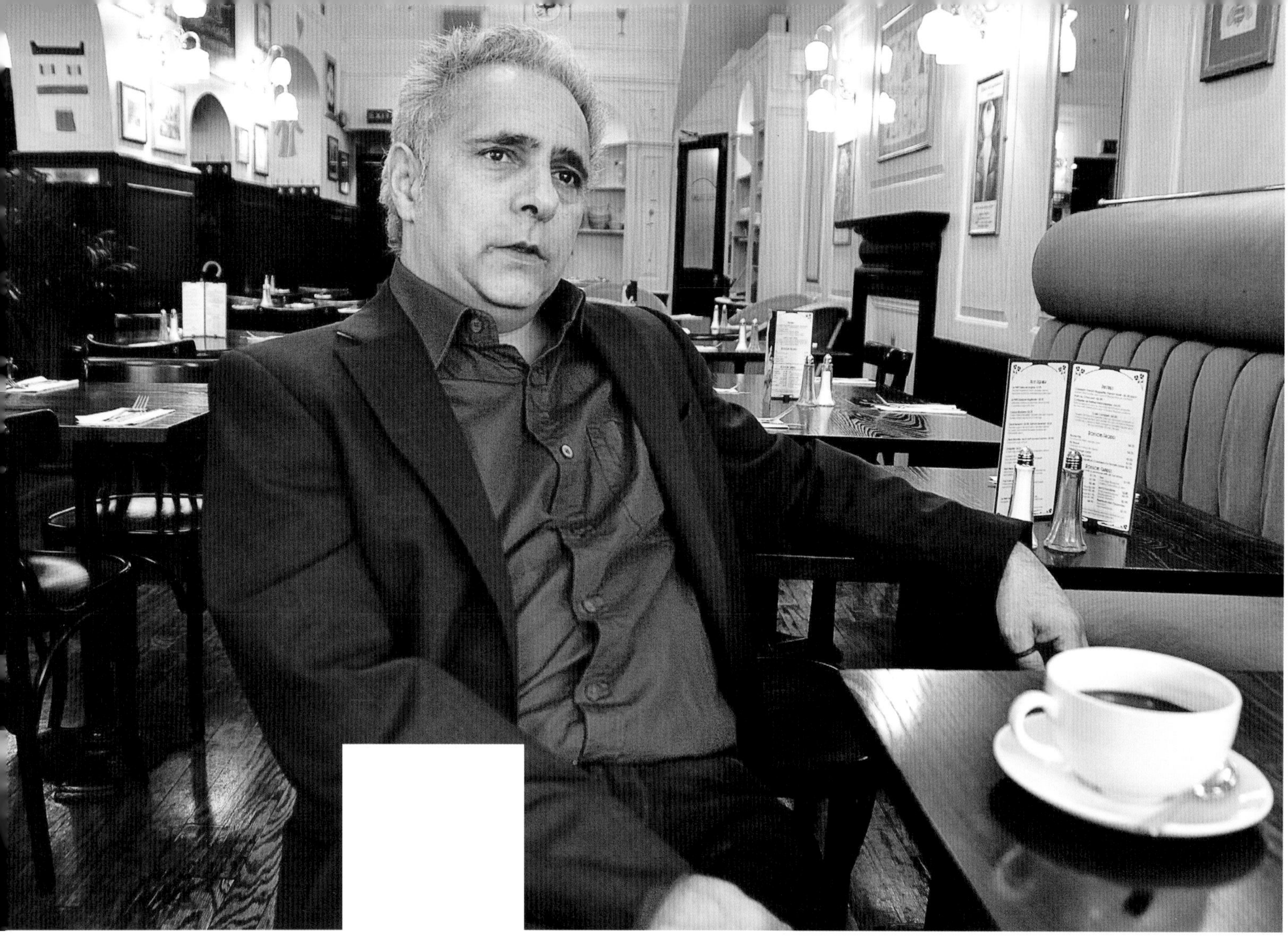

hopeless. Anyone can publish something and put it on the net, but it doesn't follow that anyone's going to read it. There are billions of words hanging there in eternity that nobody's paying any attention to at all. What you need is a network of distributors, bookshops, magazine editors and reviewers, the whole battery of the literary world, in order to get your work to the public.'

And what of the much-maligned publicity and sales departments? 'They have more and more influence over what is published now,' confirms Kureishi. He likens it to the movie industry. 'With a movie, you would ask the PR people if they could promote it. With books, that never happened before, but now it's very common.' Even an author as established as Kureishi receives rejections from these powerful sales departments. 'I sent off a proposal recently to a publishing house for a book I wanted to do and it went straight to the sales people, who said they couldn't sell it, so it's not going to be published.'

While not personally offended by this, Kureishi feels that the whole process is much less speculative than it once was, which filters down to would-be authors. 'It adversely effects people's imaginations,' he explains, 'because they're less likely to take a punt. The publishers are trying to make it more scientific, they're trying to find a formula, but it doesn't work because every now and then someone nobody's ever heard of comes along and writes a huge hit.'

Kureishi also warns that success comes with a price. 'Success is difficult to deal with because it changes your relationship with other people, particularly your old friends,' he reveals. 'One day I was living in a council flat and the next I was nominated for an Oscar. It makes other people envy you and some of those old relationships fall by the wayside. It can be a bit tricky. Nobody really prepares you for that.'

In spite of these negatives, it is clear that Kureishi would not swap his life as a writer for anything else, and that risks are part of the road to literary success. 'Write a lot,' he says. 'The output is where you really learn. You might have talent but you really have to develop it and it's a big deal to write a novel. And even though it may be a bad novel, writing badly is a very good idea.' ■

www.hanifkureishi.com

Farahad Zama

NOVELS

- Not All Marriages are Made in Heaven (2011)
- The Many Conditions of Love (2009)
- The Marriage Bureau for Rich People (2008)

Farahad Zama works for an investment bank in London and writes his novels in 400-word chunks on his laptop during his daily commute to his job. As soon as he gets off the train or the boat, he closes his laptop and turns his mind to his high-pressure job instead. However, having only a short time in which to write every day is no hindrance for Zama. When it comes to productivity, he tells me, the most important factor is 'the discipline of writing every single day.' Zama continues, 'You have to write daily, even if you are not in the mood or if it is not going very well. For me, writing is a great diversion - it helps me to relax.'

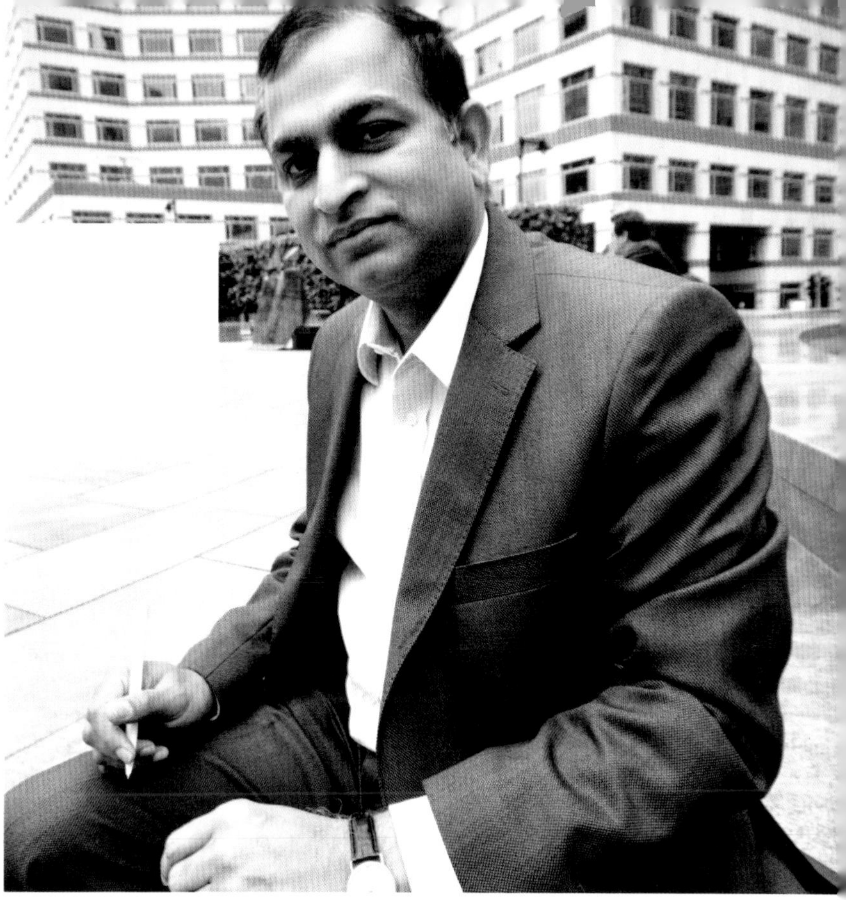

Although his début novel *The Marriage Bureau for Rich People* is often promoted as a modern Indian Cinderella story, this simple description belies its examination of many significant social issues. 'Ever since the 7/7 bombings, there has been a lot of interest in the media about how Britain failed to be a multicultural society,' he says. 'My aim was to tell a story about a country - my country, India - where multiculturalism has a much longer history than it does in Britain. In doing so, I wanted to present a different image of Muslims, away from terrorism and mirrored on my own town, Vizag, on the Eastern coast of India where people live together and share good-natured neighbourly lives in harmony.'

The Marriage Bureau explores the intricacies of arranged marriage in contemporary Indian society under the cover of humour. 'In the West,' Zama explains, 'arranged marriage equals forced marriage, which is not the case. 90% of arranged marriages are perfectly happy marriages.' Farahad Zama, himself, had an arranged marriage to Sameera, a local Vizag girl. 'How could you marry somebody you did not know?' is a common question the couple is often asked. With his novel, Farahad wants to offer the West an insight into Indian cultural and religious way of life and, simultaneously an answer to that question.

Interestingly, Zama's chief character, Mr Ali of *The Marriage Bureau*, has sometimes been compared to his fellow Little-Brown-published author Alexander McCall Smith's Mma Ramotswe of the No.1 Ladies' Detective Agency. When I ask Zama if he ever gets irritated by the analogy, he responds with a smile. 'No, not at all. In fact, McCall Smith inspired me with his style, his characters' warmth and his stories of ordinary people going on their ordinary lives.'

Zama is an avid reader of all types of books, before becoming a novelist, he would read two to three books a week. 'I got my inspiration from reading novels by R.K. Narayan or Dick Francis,' he recalls. Nowadays, however, his reading has dwindled somewhat. 'Young writers should be aware that writing strengthens your analytical faculties for how a story is constructed,' he says, 'and that can really spoil the ending for you.'

Zama's transition from reader to writer was a fairly easy one. At the start of his career, he was unaware of the mechanics of the publishing industry, so he sent his manuscript to three agents. One agent answered, and in turn sent the book out to twelve publishers, three of which were interested. Out of those companies, Zama and his new agent decided upon Little, Brown to publish his books. 'Choosing a publisher was quite simple,' he says. 'If I had a piece of advice for new writers, I would say, "Don't worry too much about which publisher is offering the highest advance, but give priority to the team that demonstrates the most enthusiasm." It is very important that the whole publishing house is behind your book because you are forging a relationship which is going to last; this is not a flash in the pan.'

In addition to finding the right publisher, Zama says, good publicity is another key factor in achieving success. 'It is difficult to publish your first book, so getting publicity is very important. For example, my first book's publication date was brought forward by six months for Richard and Judy's Book of the Year Award, and that made a huge difference.'

While the boost in sales was a welcome development, nothing was sweeter for Zama than the reception he received at a reading at the Vizag Rotary Club, where the audience included his proud parents and family. 'I did not think that Indian readers would be interested in my work, since my stories are so familiar to their everyday life, but the book was sixth on the best seller list in Delhi,' he tells me.

In spite of the difficulties, writing seems to bring Zama a lot of joy. This is only reinforced at the end of our interview, when he hands me his mobile phone to read a new message from one of his readers expressing concern about Mr Ali's son and thanking Zama for bringing some light relief to her day. ■

http://www.farahadzama.com

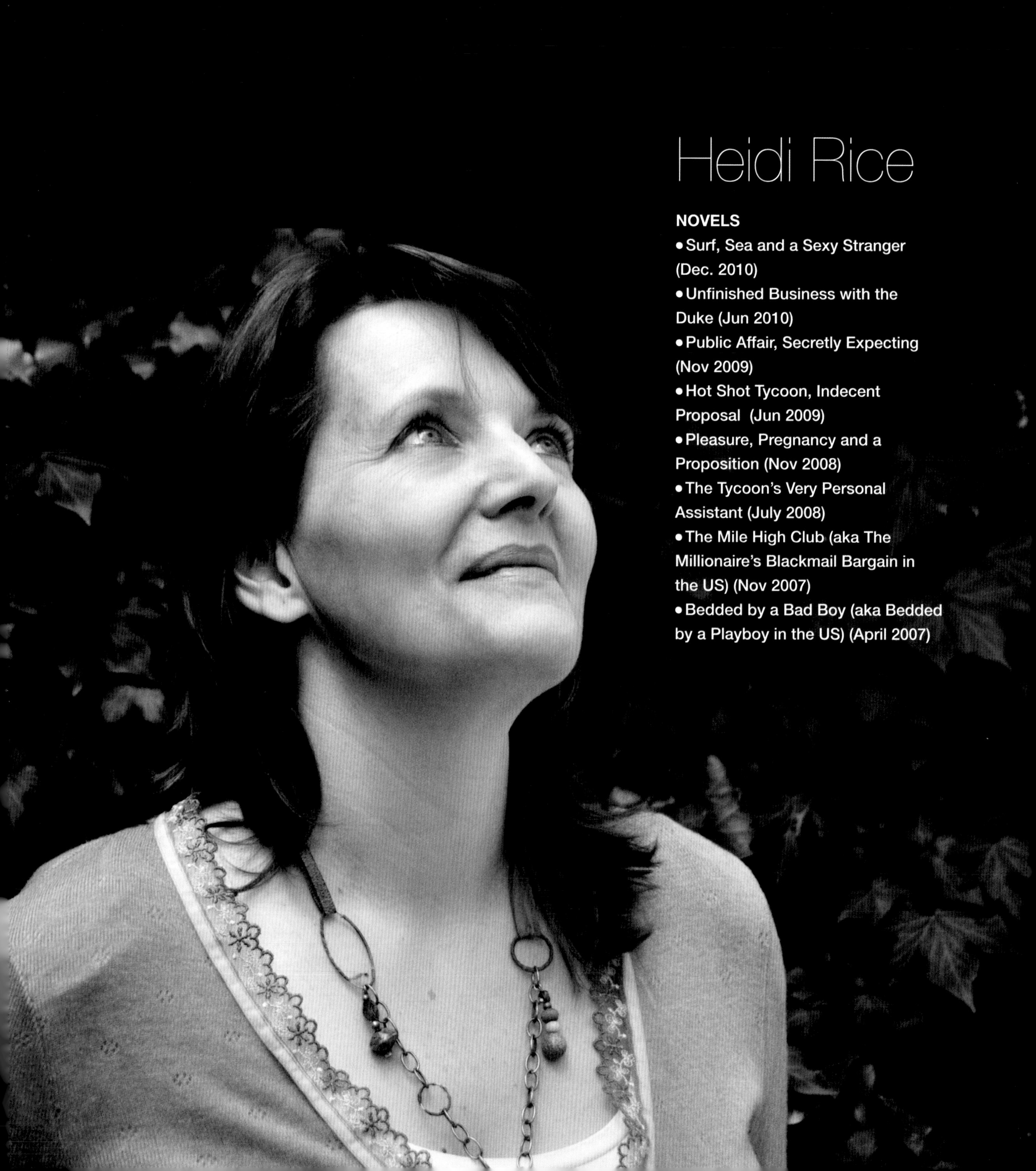

Heidi Rice

NOVELS

- Surf, Sea and a Sexy Stranger (Dec. 2010)
- Unfinished Business with the Duke (Jun 2010)
- Public Affair, Secretly Expecting (Nov 2009)
- Hot Shot Tycoon, Indecent Proposal (Jun 2009)
- Pleasure, Pregnancy and a Proposition (Nov 2008)
- The Tycoon's Very Personal Assistant (July 2008)
- The Mile High Club (aka The Millionaire's Blackmail Bargain in the US) (Nov 2007)
- Bedded by a Bad Boy (aka Bedded by a Playboy in the US) (April 2007)

Famed romance publisher Mills & Boon, which celebrated its centenary in 2008, has teamed up with the National Trust to launch a series of racy novels set in stately homes. The result is an increase in digital sales by 57% last year, while selling a copy every three seconds. Romance, it seems, is far from dead.

With this in mind, I asked Heidi Rice, one of Mills & Boon's authors, for some thoughts on the role of romance writing in the modern literary world.

'It is a niche market,' Heidi says. 'If you think that writing romance is a quick and easy way to make money, don't bother. Personally, I would say that it is a bit condescending to expect that readers are going to be fooled - romance readers know exactly what they like.' She also notes that Mills & Boon introduce new reads every month and are keen to attract new writing talent. 'You don't have to have an agent and they will read everything.'

A former freelance critic, Heidi Rice reviewed TV films for the Daily Mail until the newspaper dispensed with all its freelance reviewers. Fortunately, by then she had already sold a book to Mills & Boon. 'I've read romance since my teens. I had started a few manuscripts and when I eventually completed one, I submitted it to a publisher. After waiting eight months for a reply, I got a one line rejection letter.'

This rejection, however, was also an opportunity. Heidi discovered that 'there is a fantastic network in place for romantic novelists. I subscribed to The Romantic Novelists' Association and joined their New Writers' Scheme. I would advise writers to sign up quickly as every year they look at 250 manuscripts. They pair you up with a published author in your category, which is very useful, as a new writer is often at a loss as to where to look for specific advice. They will point out the right publishers for you and might fast-track your manuscript, and on top of it all, they will produce a detailed report of your manuscript.'

This subscription helped to launch Heidi's new career. Her Association-appointed mentor advised her to try submitting her manuscript to Mills & Boon's new Modern Heat line. 'I had not realised that I was knocking at the wrong door,' she says, with a little smile. 'My biggest problem was that my manuscript contained too much sex for the line I was originally looking at.' With book number eight on the way, she has never looked back.

According to Heidi, this type of romance is inextricably linked to the kind of sex scenes she is at ease writing. 'My sex scenes are like action scenes. They mark emotional progression. It is hard to write about relationships without including the sexual part of the relationship.' She does tell me that some of Mills & Boon's other lines, 'stop at the bedroom door,' but swiftly adds, 'You still want these scenes to be erotic, because they play a part in selling the book.'

This 'emotional progression' is similarly important outside of sex. 'The romance is only compelling if you craft the relationships carefully. The conflict between the characters is a really important part of the book. What keeps these two characters apart has to be believable - that is what drives the story.'

Heidi Rice's gripping stories attract readers from all walks of life. She strives to write both for 'people who may be educated above degree level' as well as 'people whose first language is not English.' Part of her success is due to the careful research that goes into crafting her plots and characters. For example, for the opening chapter of her upcoming book, *Surf, Sea and a Sexy Stranger*, she asked a professional lifeguard to read through the opening rescue scene to make sure all the nautical details were correct. 'You want to ground your characters in enough realism to make them believable,' she explains.

In addition to her tireless romance writing, Heidi Rice maintains a blog where she talks about issues related to being a professional author. 'I talk about how hard it is when there are a lot of revisions to do. The editor will tell you what is not working, but leaves it to you to find a solution.' She uses her latest book, *Unfinished Business With the Duke*, as an example. 'I was doing a reunion so I started the relationship from the middle. But I had focused too much on the past conflicts and the current plot was boring, so I had to rewrite that part of the story.'

Though writing can be a rewarding profession, Heidi warns, it ▶

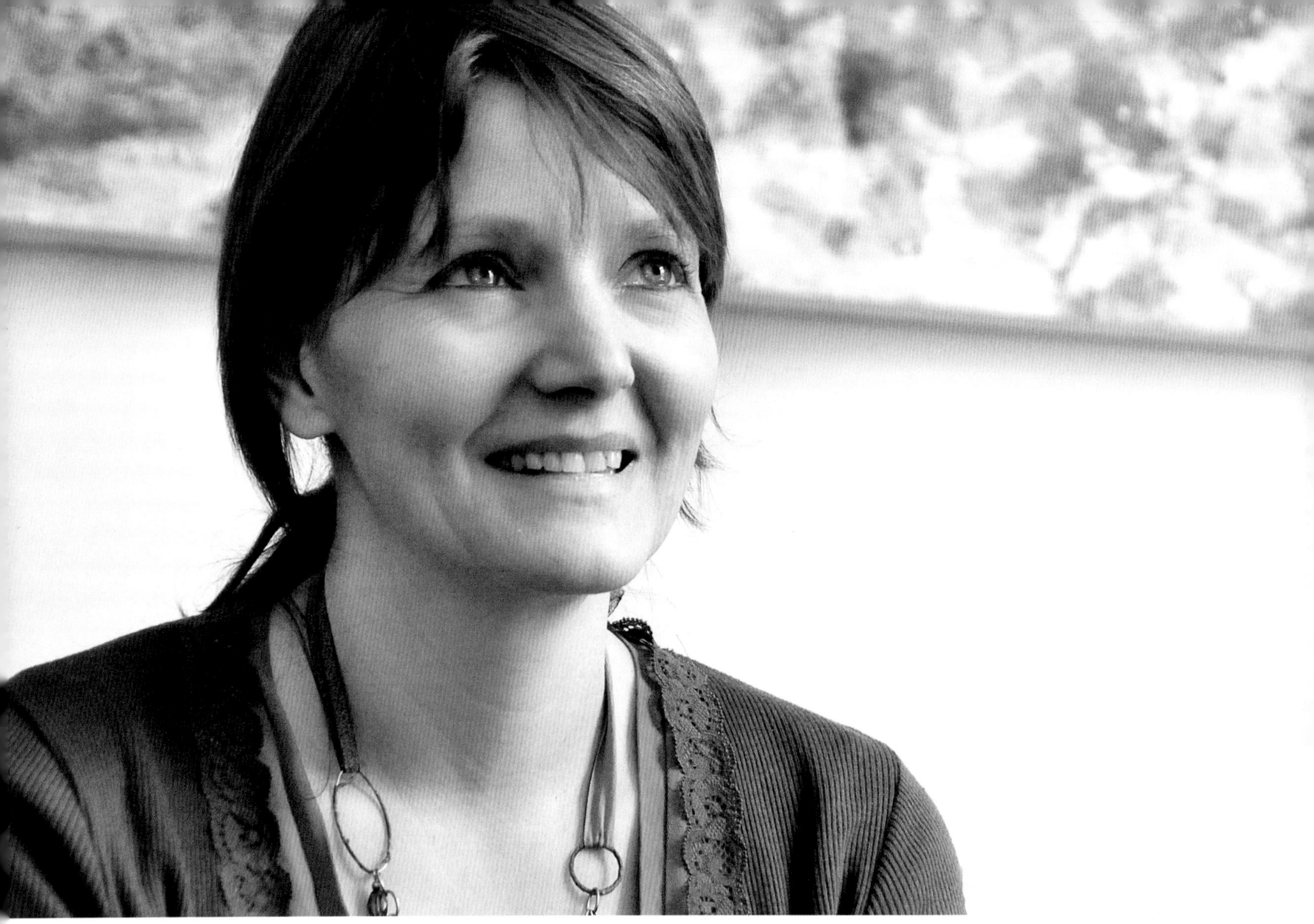

is also fraught with difficulties. 'It is so hard to make a real living from it. You won't make a lot of money for each novel, so you have to produce a lot of books. Until you have sold a book, you are not making earnings out of it. You have to treat it as a hobby and a professional occupation at the same time.'

Writers also need to learn to deal with rejection, which is often inevitable. 'You have to be able to accept rejection; it's such a competitive industry. Harlequin Mills & Boon receives over 1600 manuscripts every year of which only a very few authors are published.'

Additionally, writers need to be aware of their readers' expectations. 'There is so much to learn about writing. It is your craft which will make you a published author, especially with genre fiction like romance or crime, where people are expecting a certain kind of read and something which is easy to read.'

Most importantly, aspiring romance authors should remember Heidi Rice's number one rule: 'Love reading it.' ■

http://www.heidi-rice.com/

Jeffrey Lewis

WORKS

- Adam the King(2008)
- Theme Song for an Old Show(2007)
- Meritocracy: A Love Story(2005),
- The Conference of the Birds(2005)
- Screenwriter on *Hill Street Blues.*

Jeffrey Lewis started writing creatively at the age of nine, when his parents split up and his father moved to another state. He thinks (he's not entirely sure) that he began sending short stories to his father to gain his attention. 'It's interesting that I'm not 100% sure it's true,' he muses. 'But there's a strong possibility that I was doing it to hold my idea of a family together.'

He maintains that he was not a creative child, and after those few short stories written for an absent father, Lewis put away his pen. He wrote, he insists, just a couple of pieces in high school. 'Mostly I just wanted to be liked in high school,' he says with a smile and a shrug. And despite a similar attitude to his Yale years, Lewis did write for the Yale Literary Review and won a poetry competition to become Class Poet (that same year, John Kerry was Class Orator).

By the time he left Yale, Lewis had plans to be a writer. But the Vietnam War was raging and the draft beckoned, and as he 'wasn't that interested in participating,' he went to teach in Greece before returning to America to study law at Harvard. "I had to do something constructive to stay out of the draft,' he says, 'and law qualified. Being a writer did not.'

Armed with an office-grade electric typewriter and knowledge gathered from creative writing classes, Lewis left Harvard and wrote his first novel. 'I couldn't get it published,' he recalls; in fact, his desk drawers began to fill up with countless drafts of unpublished manuscripts. 'I wasn't pleased. It's not a lot of fun to hear that everything you've done is for naught. And it never occurred to me that you could be an older writer; I thought it was only possible to be a young writer and if you weren't successful when you were young, there was no point.' He laughs as he thinks of his younger, more idealistic self. 'I suppose I felt I was a great new voice coming along and I had better get out there while I was still a great new voice.'

As the rejections mounted, Lewis began to feel increasingly isolated and his writing became progressively more obscure, so he decided to take his career in a different direction and seek out what all writers fear: a 'real' job. A part-time research job made him something of an expert on organized crime in New York and led to a stint at the District Attorney's office in Manhattan. However, this actually directed him back to writing; when Lewis subsequently moved to California, he landed a writing job on Hill Street Blues, a crime drama set in New York. 'Thanks to my work as an assistant DA, I guess knew more than almost anyone else in Hollywood about how crime worked in New York at that moment.'

Lewis worked on the show for most of its seven-season run, winning a couple of Emmys in the process. But hearing fiction call to him once more, he set about writing a novel. Years of writing for TV had matured Lewis as a writer and taught him to pay attention to his audience in a way he hadn't as a younger author, but things still took time. 'I think I have a long germination process. It takes a long time for me to find a voice - any voice! But once I do, I tend to go pretty fast ▶.

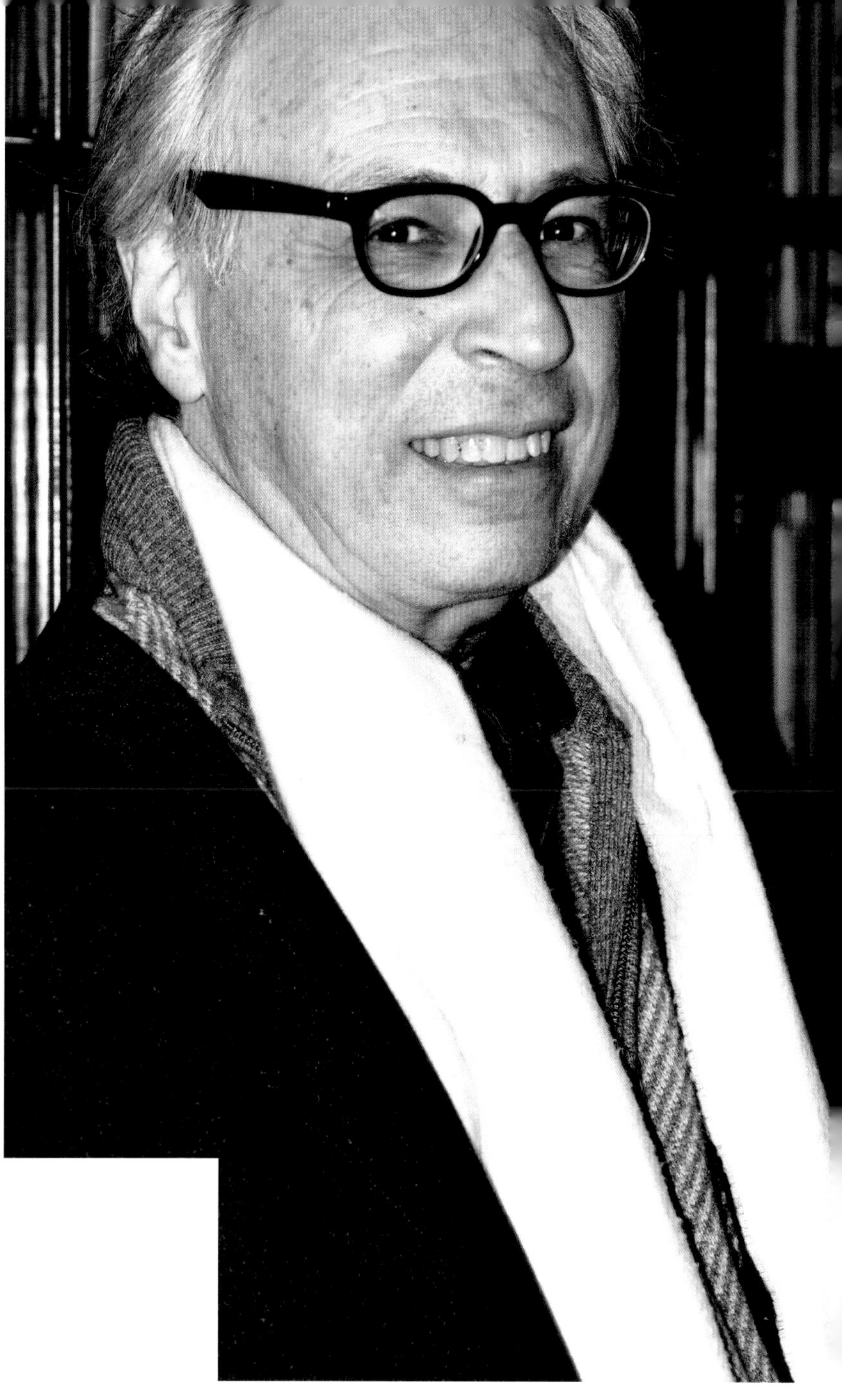

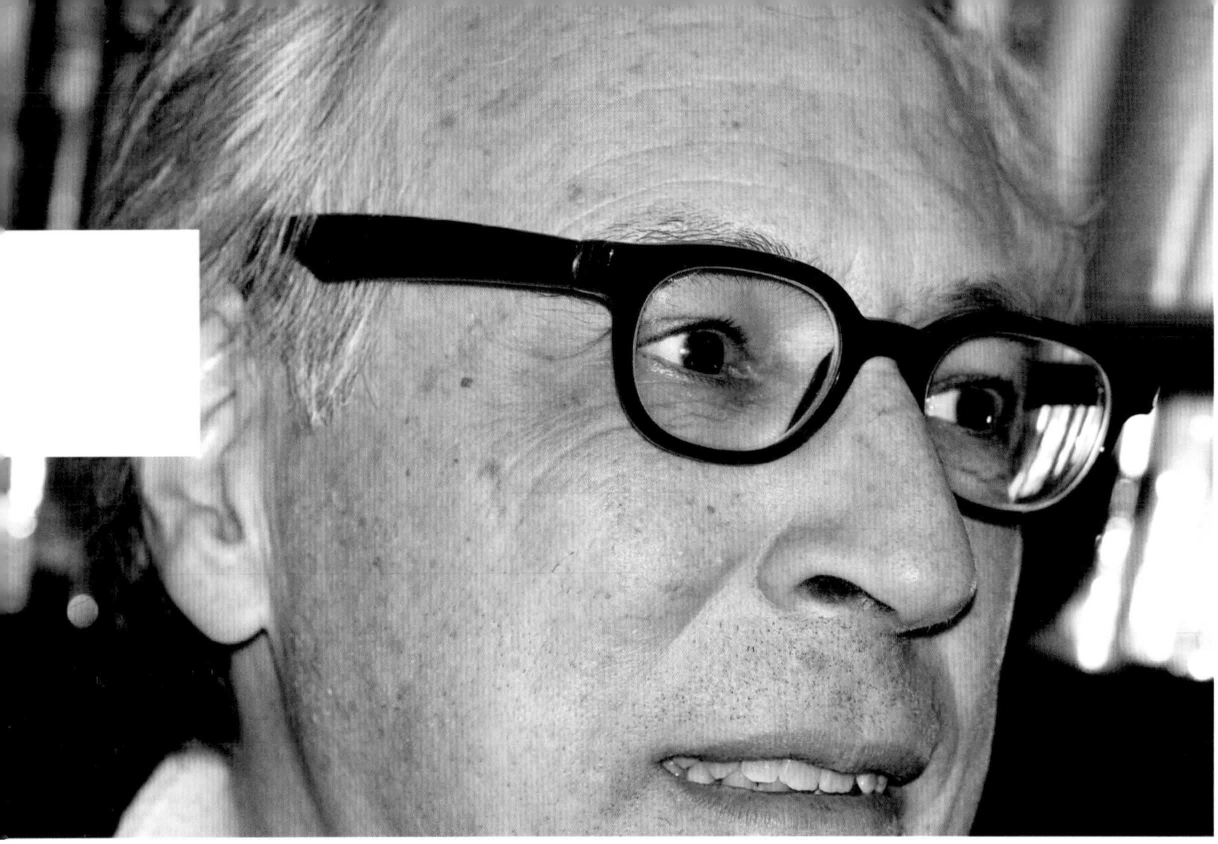

I think I wrote each of my books over the course of a couple of months.'

I ask him if he has ever suffered from writer's block. He looks troubled. 'I'm not sure, because I'm not sure exactly what people mean. I think from the way people talk about it, no. But I'm not naturally facile, so you could call that writer's block. I don't sit down in the morning and just throw up pages worth of stuff. I face a lot of resistance when I write; it seems to be part of the process.'

The day that Lewis finished the first draft of *Meritocracy: a Love Story,* he was invited to a party thrown by his friend Barbara Epstein, the then editor of the New York Review of Books. He took his seventeen-year-old daughter Sarah along with him, and buoyed by an appreciative glance she received from Leonardo DiCaprio in the hotel lobby, she started conversing with a publisher, whom she then introduced to her father. 'I was pretty full of myself at this point,' Lewis recalls, 'because I thought my invitation was a pretty good coincidence and I felt good because nobody had told me my book was bad or they weren't interested. It was a moment of total hope.'

He still marvels at his lucky break. 'They always say that to get published as a writer you have to get an agent, but in order to get an agent you have to have sold something, so it's impossible. You have to try and cut what is essentially that Gordian knot of impossibility.'

Lewis is very aware of the serendipitous nature of his path to success. Writing is, he says, 'a very lucky thing to be able to do. You get to say what you think, you get to not wake up too early, you get away without having to work with anyone that resembles a boss, and you get to think you can make the world a little better, or at least a little more bearable, for people.'

One downside to writing, Lewis feels, is the lack of publicity available to fiction authors in America today. But despite that, he refuses to jump on the bandwagon and promote himself on Facebook or Twitter. 'I probably should, but I won't,' he grimaces. 'Facebook in particular. As a writer I hate their abuse of the word "friend" – I protest by being a non-participant.'

Of course, another difficult aspect of earning a living from writing is that 'it's hard to get away with it, hard to figure out how it can be done.' There's a long pause. 'I'm not sure. I feel like I should warn young writers that people aren't reading these things anymore, but that seems too negative. Why put someone off something that's actually very important for the world?' He considers his next words carefully. 'The only thing to do is to write. There's no external criterion that determines whether you're a writer or not - it's only whether you've done it.' ■

Find out more at www.jeffreylewis-novels.com

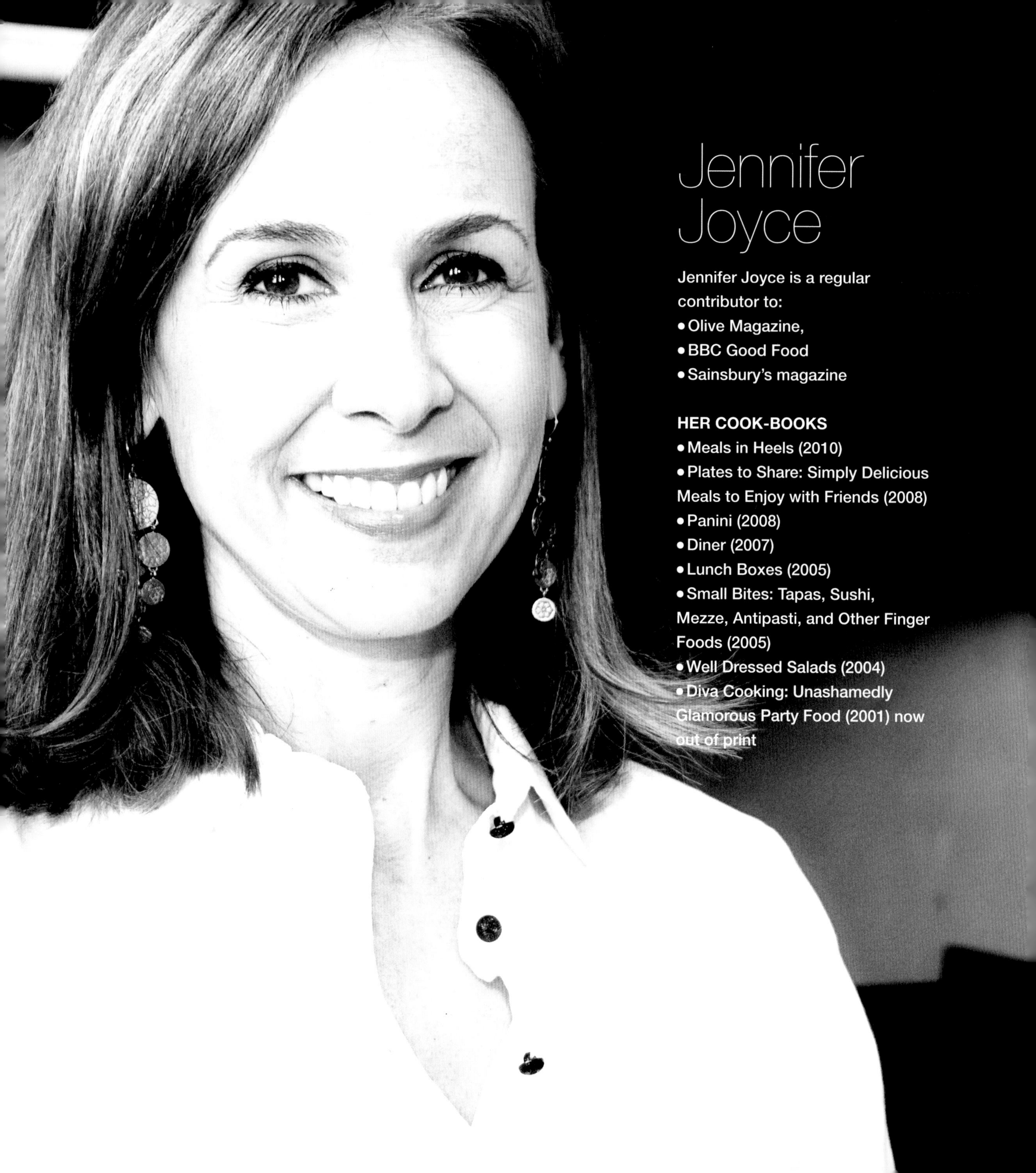

Jennifer Joyce

Jennifer Joyce is a regular contributor to:

- Olive Magazine,
- BBC Good Food
- Sainsbury's magazine

HER COOK-BOOKS

- Meals in Heels (2010)
- Plates to Share: Simply Delicious Meals to Enjoy with Friends (2008)
- Panini (2008)
- Diner (2007)
- Lunch Boxes (2005)
- Small Bites: Tapas, Sushi, Mezze, Antipasti, and Other Finger Foods (2005)
- Well Dressed Salads (2004)
- Diva Cooking: Unashamedly Glamorous Party Food (2001) now out of print

Jennifer Joyce's journey began in her childhood home. 'I have a half-Italian, half-Polish family background, and I am the youngest of 9 children. At home, everything was cooked from scratch and we all helped in the kitchen. As a child, I read a lot of cookbooks. I could not wait to be at that level so that I could make this or that recipe. It was something to aspire to, something to reach for.'

'After finishing with school, I went into business. Then, I spent six months travelling all over Europe exploring various cuisines. When I went to Italy, I felt I had arrived. I felt at one with the people, with the way they ate. After reading all those cookbooks when I was a child, I thought that I had arrived home.'

'Then when I moved to London and looked for a job, I was given a cooking slot at the Books for Cooks store, where fellow chef Victoria Blashford-Snell and I rapidly became friends – we had a lot of synergy as cooks. I helped her with her catering business, sometimes working until 2 o'clock in the morning.'

It was during this time that Jennifer Joyce began to think about writing a cookbook. 'Victoria Blashford-Snell was already a published food-writer, she told me that if I got a publisher and wrote a proposal, she would do a book with me. This is how I got a foot in the door and we published *Diva Cooking: Unashamedly Glamorous Party Food*.'

What does Jennifer believe a food writer needs to do to succeed?

"To get published,' she tells me, 'it helps if you are connected to a name that publishers will recognise - for example, a writer who has worked with them before - and it is very important to send in the right proposal. At Books for Cooks almost everyone had been published, so they helped me to write my proposal. But I still approached about fifteen publishers before *Diva Cooking* got printed. Writers also need feedback and need to take their time. My last book took two years to put together.'

Jennifer then lets me in on the secret of how she creates her recipes. 'I stay home for a week during which I have a giant brainstorm. I develop recipes surrounded by hundreds of books and clippings that give me tons of ideas, which I then discuss with my publisher. Nothing is ever a waste of time to develop. All the experimentations I do are used either for classes I teach or for other magazines. I make notes, being very thorough with the measurements. I write my recipes on the computer so that I can come back to them as I test them. I am fanatical about testing. I test a lot. You really have to test your recipes at least twice. I cook each recipe twice - once at home and then in a class – before it goes into a book.'

When I ask for some final words, she leaves me with an even stronger sense of her deep love for food and cooking. 'My books are for all cooks who want to learn something new. To me, food is a source of comfort and happiness. I think that I can always walk into the kitchen and make something in it which will take me back to a happy place. It calls back memories of my childhood, when the eleven of us were in the kitchen preparing dinner. Cooking is like coming home.' ■

To read more about Jennifer Joyce and her work, visit her website at http://www.jenniferjoyce.co.uk/

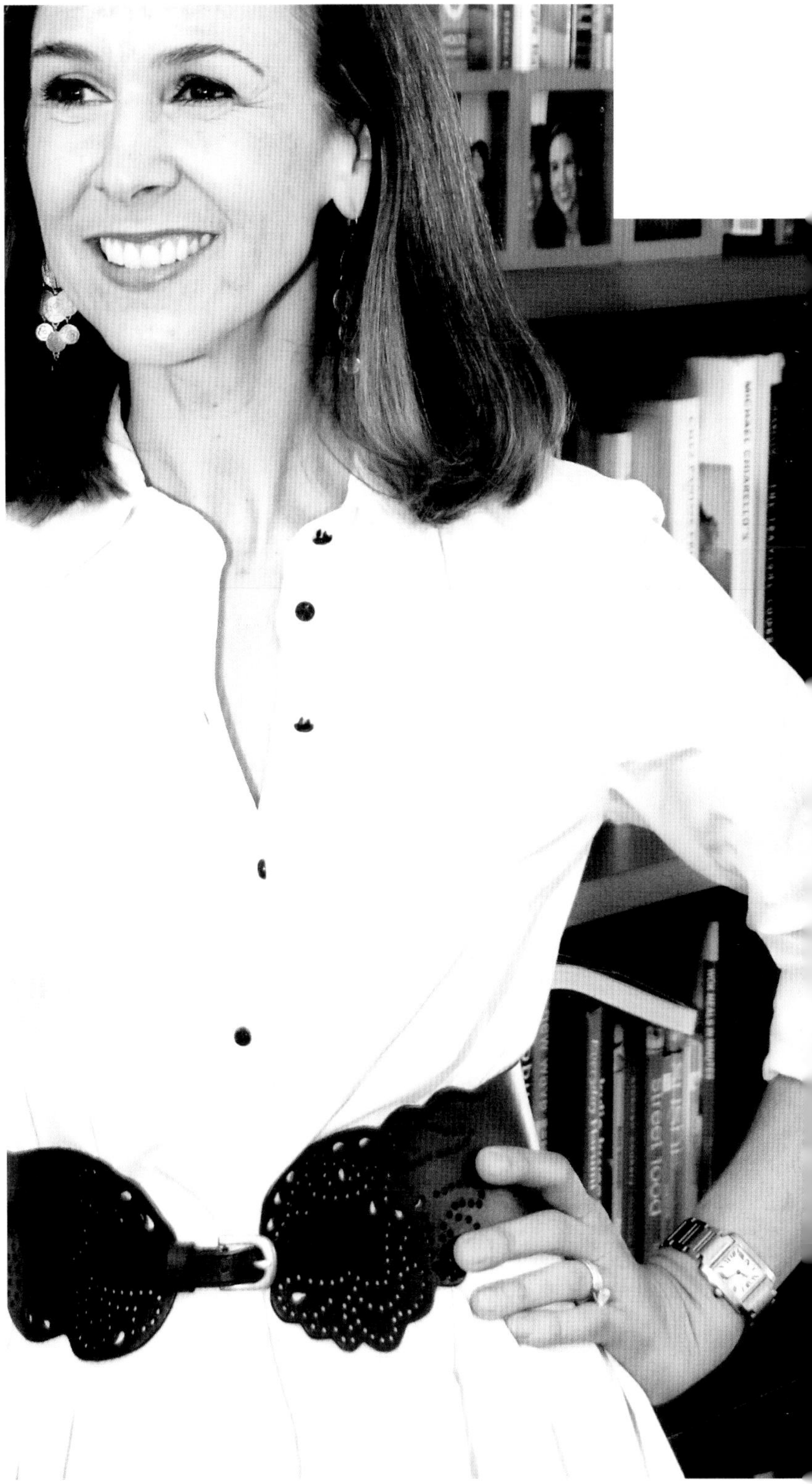

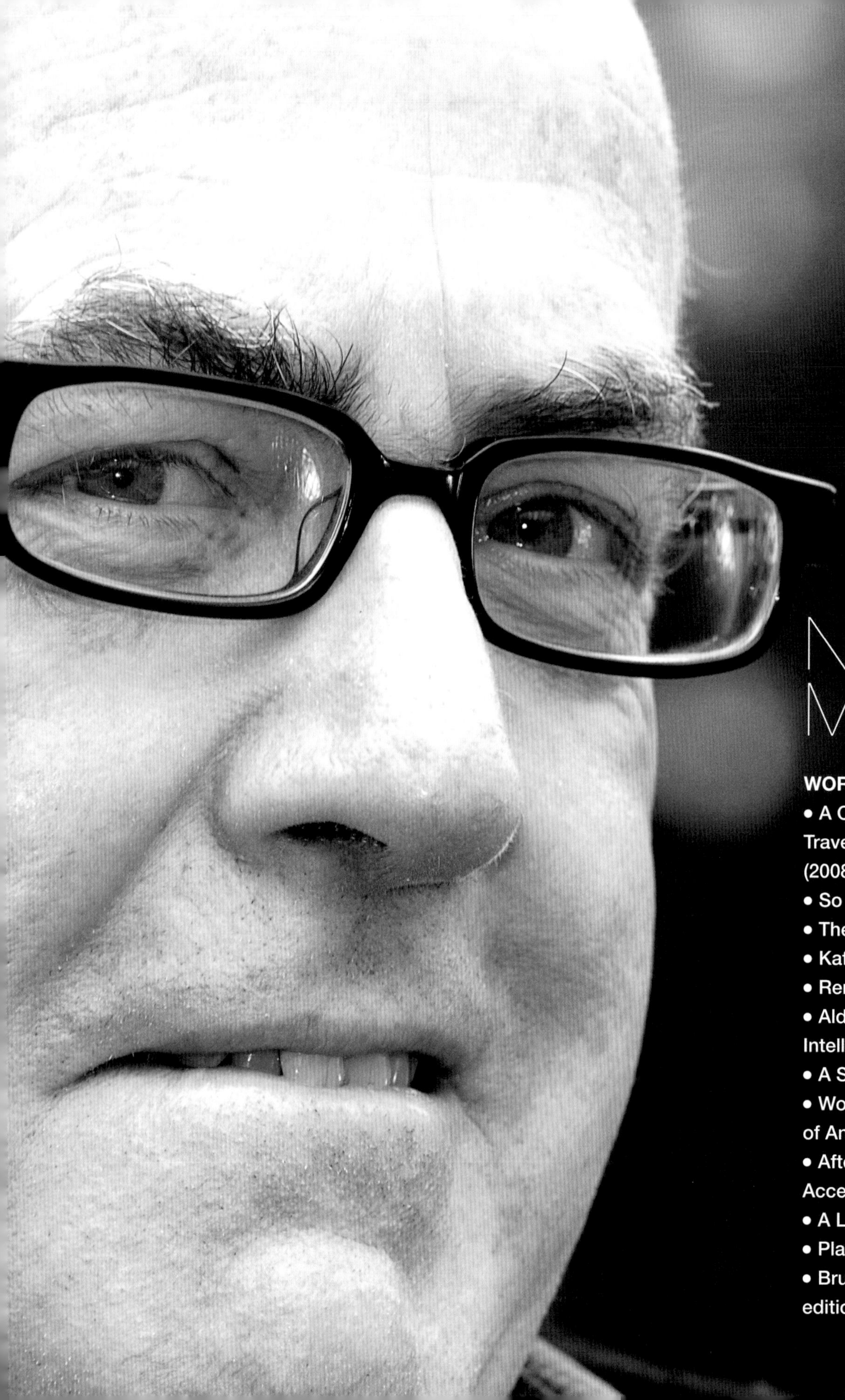

Nicholas Murray

WORKS

- A Corkscrew is Most Useful: The Travellers of Empire Spirited a Town (2008)
- So Spirited a Town (2007)
- The Narrators (2006)
- Kafka (2004)
- Remembering Carmen (2003)
- Aldous Huxley: an English Intellectual (2002)
- A Short Book About Love (2001)
- World Enough and Time: The Life of Andrew Marvell (1999)
- After Arnold: Culture and Accessibility (1997)
- A Life of Matthew Arnold (1996)
- Plausible Fictions (1995)
- Bruce Chatwin (1993) (revised edition with new afterword, 1995)

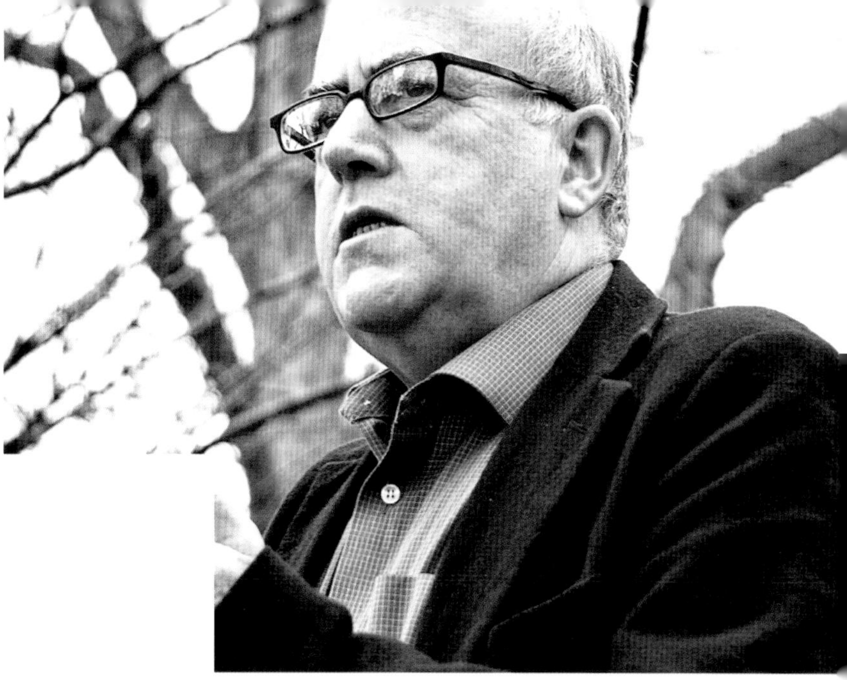

Just before turning 40, Nicholas Murray had a unique opportunity. He received a letter from the poet and critic John Powell Ward, who was editing a series called Borderlines. The series focused on the landscape of the Welsh Marches and the writers associated with that region. Ward was looking for an author to write a volume on Bruce Chatwin. For Murray, this was the chance of a lifetime.

His biography of Chatwin was an instant success. Since then, Nicholas has not stopped writing. With a book published every year, he is a full time writer.

Nicholas Murray has regular working habits. When he researches a biography, he clocks on at the British Library at 9.30. He writes his best in the morning, and thinks that the art of concentration is of utter importance for the writing process. He might attach a psychological importance to the objects in front of him to create an conducive atmosphere but certainly advises budding authors to set up a writing space where they feel comfortable. He does not wish to be a prophet of doom, but he is very concerned about what the future holds for writers.

If you were asked what one requires to be a successful writer what would you say?

Talent, and luck. A combination of meeting the right person at the right moment when you are ready. When I wrote Bruce Chatwin, he had just died and everybody was interested in him, he was very fashionable. On the strength of that I took my short biography to an agent who asked me what I would like to do next, I pondered and said: "I would quite like to do Arnold". The next day, the very same agent went to lunch with a publisher. The latter had been an undergraduate at Oxford where he had written a dissertation on Matthew Arnold and within 4 days the deal was sewn up. After years and years of persevering, suddenly the ice melted but of course I was asked in the first place because people in the trade thought that I could do it.

What is the attraction of writing poetry?

If you have a day to yourself, may be you can write a whole poem. You do poetry for its own sake, you do it for love or just because you like doing it. Nobody gets any money out of writing poetry. Even a well-known poet like Seamus Heaney gets his earnings from related activities, he had a job teaching poetry at Harvard University. Poetry is beautiful, poetry is above all the horrible business ethic, it is just pure art.

What are the biggest hurdles faced by writers?

Rejections, lots of rejections. Oh! By the way, poetry teaches you the art of accepting magazines' rejections. When one starts sending work off to magazines, rejections are more frequent than acceptances. Rejection can be depressing because you never know if the fault is with you or with them.

As for biographies, publishers are becoming more reluctant to commission traditional literary biography : the life of one writer. Nowadays, they prefer group biographies. The offers are controlled by the sales and marketing people and the moment they say: "It is not going to sell, nobody is interested" it becomes a self-fulfilling prophecy.

It could even get worse because the price of books is falling. There is a developing culture of getting free content. Ebooks will force the price down and there will be less money for the writers. Writers write because they are driven; you have to be inspired when you are writing otherwise the reader will get bored but also you need an advance large enough to sustain you while you are doing the work and that in time might disappear.

Do you have any tips for all the budding writers out there?

- Maintain a presence. I do it with my website and I write a blog.
- Get a publishing advance which is large enough to sustain you full time while you are writing.
- There are no rules about writing methods. Do what appeals to you. If you like writing pencil on paper then do it. I don't attach any mystical significance in the medium, but some things matter, such as you might work at a particular desk or have a certain object which creates the atmosphere.
- If you chose to be a biographer, you will spend more time researching than writing.
- Be aware of distractions. I can write anywhere, people might be drilling outside it does not matter, but if the phone rings that is it. I don't need silence, I need concentration. How are you going to write a 120 thousand word book in a given time unless you concentrate and have regular habits.
- Don't dabble. Writers are professionals which means that they must deliver the goods.
- Make sure your publisher farms your work out to a good editor.
- Relish good writing and it will rub off. In the words of Jorge Luis Borges "good readers are even blacker and rarer swans than good writers". How could you compose a piece of music if you never listen to any? ■

About the author : http://www.nicholasmurray.co.uk

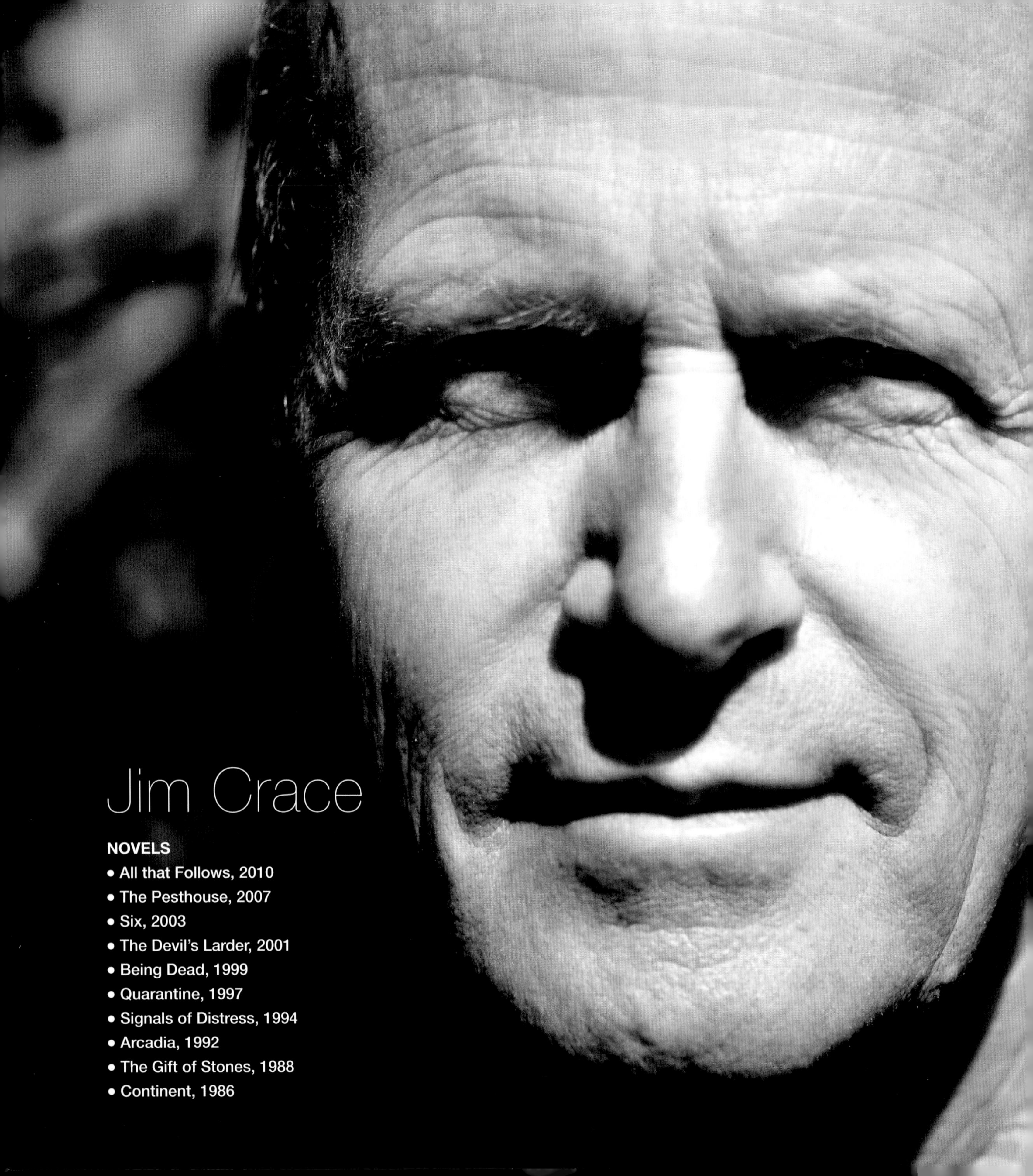

Jim Crace

NOVELS

- All that Follows, 2010
- The Pesthouse, 2007
- Six, 2003
- The Devil's Larder, 2001
- Being Dead, 1999
- Quarantine, 1997
- Signals of Distress, 1994
- Arcadia, 1992
- The Gift of Stones, 1988
- Continent, 1986

Jim Crace is said to be a secretive person, a mystery and he doesn't include many life details in his books either. He came to fiction from a successful career in journalism, but beyond that, not much more is widely known.

'Why did you sign your first book contract?' I asked. 'After sixteen thriving years in journalism, you could have carried on.'

'I have always been a storyteller,' said the author, 'but I ended up in journalism. I was a very puritanical journalist. I never dared make anything up, yet what that meant was that my desire to invent things was suppressed. So I started to write short pieces of fiction on the side, only I never expected that I could make a living from it.'

He takes a sip of coffee, humour briefly flashing in his eyes. 'I knew that most writers either a) either did not get published, b) nobody read their works except for their cousins, so if you were a Catholic, you did better than anybody else because you had more cousins or c) even if you were published and well-regarded and had good critical response, you did not make any money. So I had an ambition to write fiction but I never, for one second, believed that it would be a career for me.'

In 1974, Jim Crace published the realist fantasy story, *Annie, Californian Plates*,' which garnered him a lot of attention. Publishers, agents, and others were phoning him and asking if he had written a novel, or even if they could pay him to write a novel. So what did he do next?

'Of course, as a freelance journalist, I never said no to any money,' Jim Crace recalls. 'I was offered a small advance of £1500. So when I signed the contract, I was flattered, but still I did not expect to make any money.'

He started a political novel, only it felt heavy and dead on the page. 'I did not know what the end of the next sentence was, let alone what the end of the book would add up to,' says he. 'It was not my natural voice.' His troubles were compounded by the collapse of his journalistic life. A new editor-in-chief had taken over the Telegraph, her idea of the perfect article was 'The Rise and Fall of the Shoulder Pad.' Serious journalism was being replaced by celebrity journalism, pushing Crace's professional work into irrelevance and he still had not found his voice as a novelist.

One day, completely by chance, he was asked to review a poorly translated Gabriel Garcia Marquez book, In Evil Hour. Though it was far from Marquez's best, it hit him like a bolt from the blue. 'Reading it, I recognized my own voice. It was as if I had been singing contralto when I was really a soprano. A magical realistic voice which did not wear its heart on its sleeve or fly a political banner, but looked at the world obliquely, and not through the clear glass of realism.' This realisation led him to write his first novel, *Continent*, which won three awards even before publication. Jim Crace's story is atypical in the world of contemporary writing: his books never received a single rejection only prizes and awards.

I bring up my last key point: advice for budding writers.

'I don't think reading is the key to writing,' Crace says, contradicting the conventional wisdom shared by most writers. He explains, 'I know that it is very fashionable to say that if you want to become a writer, read, read, read and then write from your own experience. I would say don't read, read, read; live, live, live. In all of my books there are a lot of landscapes and wildlife, but I don't write about landscapes and wildlife because I've read about them. I write about them because I do the walks and I look in the sky and I see the birds. You need to go to the first source. The important thing for writers is to have a subject that does not come from books but from your life, your own interests or from some kind of passion, from your politics or your love life. Put the book down, put your shoes on and go out.'

'If you want to become a writer, do a lot of writing. You don't become a musician by going to concerts. Don't write about your own experience, because most of us are not interesting. Some writers are very good on a sentence-by-sentence basis, but their lives are not interesting enough. There is not enough death in their lives. There is no war, not enough adultery or diseases. This is what novels need: the dark side of human nature. The important thing is to not just write about yourself, but to write about something you are really interested in and to weave your mood into the narrative.' ■

Jim Crace's last novel, his eleventh, is due to be published next year, 2011. For more information, go to: www.jim-crace.com

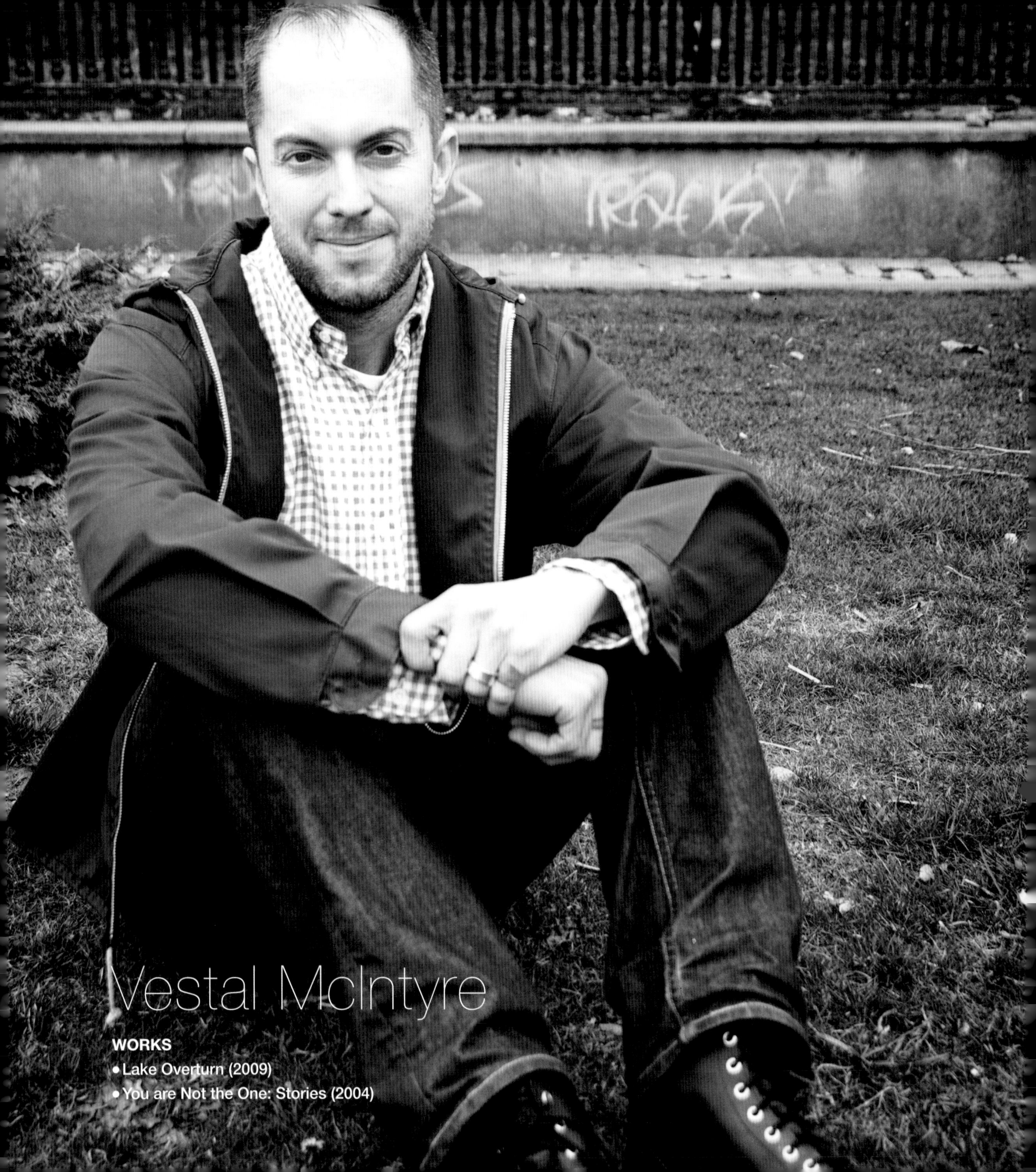

Vestal McIntyre

WORKS

- Lake Overturn (2009)
- You are Not the One: Stories (2004)

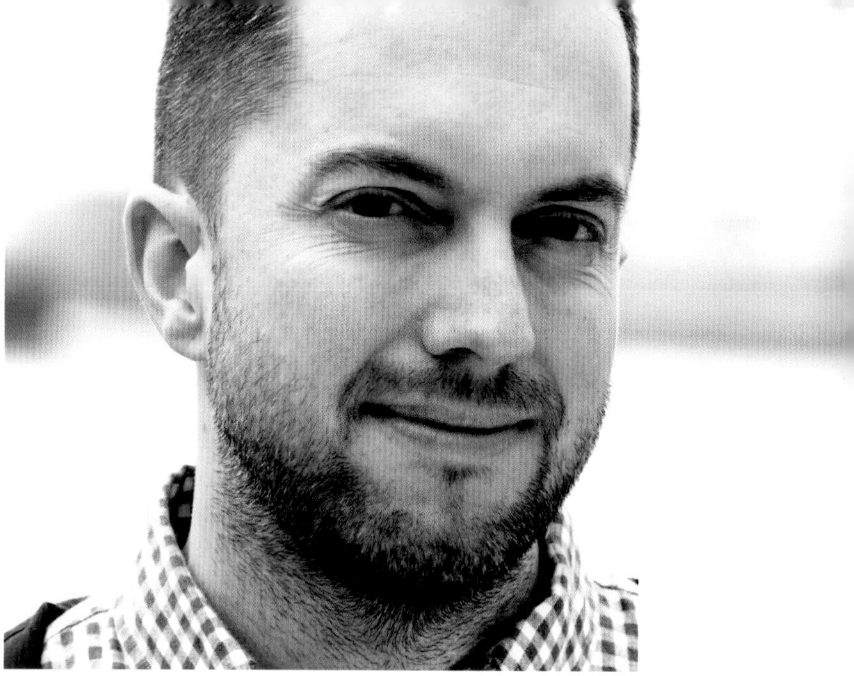

It would have been easy to mistake Vestal McIntyre for a local university student when he approached our meeting point, a bench by the Thames at Greenwich. For a man whose writing was designated Editors' Choice in the New York Times Book Review, whose first book, *You Are Not the One: Stories* was awarded a Lambda Literary Award, whose first novel, Lake Overturn, was described as the next Great American Novel, and whose entrance in the literary world was greeted by a rousing fanfare of compliment, my first impression of McIntyre is one of unpretentiousness, simplicity and natural qualities.

I start by asking him whether he'd always wanted to be a writer. 'I was always writing poems and things when I was little,' says McIntyre, 'so I wanted to be a writer pretty early, when I was eleven or twelve years old.'

His first major inspiration came, albeit indirectly, from his sister. 'When I was in junior high and my older sister was in university, she brought home an anthology from her English class in which she had marked things she thought I should read. So when I was thirteen, I read William Faulkner and Joyce Carol Oates, which was a shock because I grew up in a very religious family and went to a very conservative religious school. The things they constantly gave us to read there were the Bible and various religious testimonials, and then I started reading these really weird, challenging, interesting stories. I think that is what really made me want to be a writer.'

Does Vestal have any literary idols? 'Flannery O'Connor was also in that collection. Her story was the weirdest, most disturbing thing that I'd read, but it was also very funny. It introduced me to a new set of emotions that I didn't know you could get from reading, so I went and got her books from the library. She kind of became my hero after that.'

Inspired by these stories, McIntyre began writing a novel, which unfortunately was never printed. 'It was devastating at the time,' he recalls, 'but now I look at it and I am really glad that it was not published because it would have been really immature. I had more writing to do before I was ready.' However, he soon bounced back, writing short stories for literary magazines and eventually publishing two award-winning books.

His writing methods vary. 'When I write a short story, I've already been thinking about it for a few days or months or years. I change my method all the time to see what will happen. I get most of my new writing done early in the morning, for some reason, and in the afternoon I do the editing. When I finish a story, I never show it to people straight away. I put it aside for at least a few weeks until I can read it as a reader, not as a writer, and make it as good as I can.'

McIntyre also relies on few people for a first feedback. 'I have a small group of readers I trust who are the first to see it and then the editing happens over several months. I think writers always want to write something fantastic that everybody will love, especially when they start out. But it does not happen like that,' he laughs, 'or at least it did not happen to me.'

What does he think writers should do to improve their craft? 'I think there is something about having to spend hours and hours and hours writing. It is a skill, like learning to be a concert pianist. It's not like going on The X Factor and getting immediate praise. You have to learn all sorts of crafts and techniques in order to develop the skills needed to create fiction worthy of being read. When you are reading, you don't realise these techniques exist. There are definite mechanisms you have to employ to make your writing feel like real life and not boring drivel. You have to do things to the writing that are quite unnatural. You have to cut things way down to make them feel real.'

When I ask Vestal about the topic of self-confidence, he assures me, 'I do have confidence in my writing. I am lucky that way, even though I send out stories again and again and get rejections 90% of the time.' Instead of discarding these stories, though, he returns to them in future writing. 'Sometimes I decide to change them or send them to someone else because you never know. One man's trash is another man's treasure.'

He adds, 'Two of my best stories have been rejected by dozens of magazines; it is a matter of taste and timing. I think one of the tricks is to send so many stories, to apply for so many grants, so that the constant flow of rejections does not bother you any more, and then once in a while your work will be accepted and it will be the best thing.'

As it starts to mizzle and we wrap up our interview, McIntyre encourages authors to be open to change. 'You can't depend on the same kind of characters or you will get in a rut, always writing the same thing. You even can't depend on the same set of structures. Sometimes I write a sentence and it sounds like one of my old sentences, so I make myself change it because things have to be fresh all the time. Writing is so difficult to get out that you revert back to the kind of emotional tricks or sentences that you are used to. To grow as a writer,' he concludes, 'you have to stop yourself doing that.' ■

His website is www.vestalmcintyre.com.

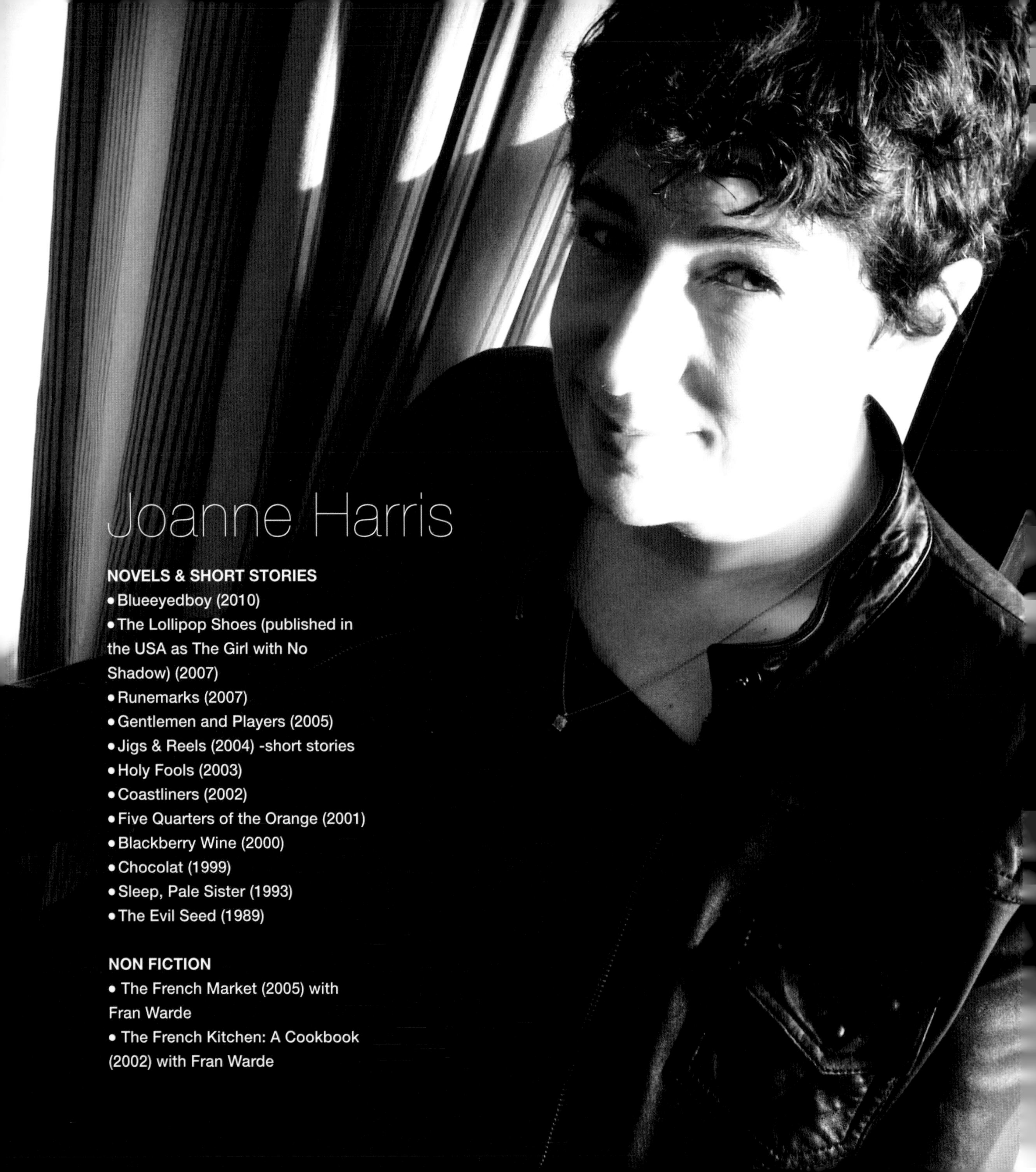

Joanne Harris

NOVELS & SHORT STORIES

- Blueeyedboy (2010)
- The Lollipop Shoes (published in the USA as The Girl with No Shadow) (2007)
- Runemarks (2007)
- Gentlemen and Players (2005)
- Jigs & Reels (2004) -short stories
- Holy Fools (2003)
- Coastliners (2002)
- Five Quarters of the Orange (2001)
- Blackberry Wine (2000)
- Chocolat (1999)
- Sleep, Pale Sister (1993)
- The Evil Seed (1989)

NON FICTION

- The French Market (2005) with Fran Warde
- The French Kitchen: A Cookbook (2002) with Fran Warde

Born in Barnsley, where her grandparents had a sweet shop, Joanne Harris' earliest memory is of 'seeing the sun shining through the jars of boiled sweets.' Who's Who lists her hobbies as 'mooching, lounging, strutting, strumming, priest-baiting and quiet subversion of the system,' while her web site notes that 'she also enjoys obfuscation, sleaze, rebellion, witchcraft, armed robbery, tea and biscuits.'

In comparison, Harris' mixed background - her mother's family is French - might not seem so noteworthy. However, she believes that her backgrounds shaped her writing by providing her with a unique linguistic awareness. 'English is not my first language,' she explains. 'The two different aspects of my background gave me a different approach to the algorithm of language, a different cultural vocabulary and a different perspective.'

Interestingly, Harris finds the French literary market particularly challenging, despite her French background and the fact that her first bestseller, *Chocolat*, is set in the tiny French village of Lansquenet-sous-Tannes. 'The French publishing industry is quite strange,' she says. 'At first they wanted me to change my name, and then they wanted me to either write about England or to be wholly French. The industry there seems to have a problem with anybody who is not perceived as French writing about France, though the general public does not have a big problem with my books.'

While *Chocolat* laid the foundation for her writing career, Harris published three books before she was able to put an end to her fifteen-year teaching career. She tells me that she would not have made a living from her first book. 'This is something that young writers don't realise. They have a perception, which is mostly media-generated, of the big break which suddenly gets you a lot of money and suddenly makes you a household name. They don't have much perception of what comes before the big break, or of the fact that, for most people, the big break does not really come. People juggle daytime jobs and writing, very often being published but not being able to make a living.'

Making a living from writing is difficult and Harris was fortunate with her publisher. 'My first two books were Gothic novels and were deeply unfashionable at the time. In the same way, when I wrote *Chocolat*, the trend was for extremely sparse writing with no adjectives, without embellishment. And I came out with this book filled with food and a style which was profoundly unfashionable. Nobody knew what to do with such a book. It was turned down dozens of times by publishers,' she adds. 'Now they refuse to acknowledge that by saying that they bid for it but did not get it. But I know. I read the rejection letters. What they really mean is that they wanted to bid for it, but were prevented from doing so by various acquisition departments because it was a risky venture. I have since found a good publisher who allows me all sorts of chances with all sorts of books – some people in publishing are still willing to take a punt at something unfashionable.'

What factors, in Harris' opinion, determine whether a book will be published? 'It is one of those things that people have to fight for repeatedly,' she says. 'So much of it is about luck and perseverance. I feel a bit sorry for so many unknown authors because the emphasis is so much on celebrities, and the budget goes so much into promoting people you have heard of.'

'It takes a certain kind of reader to choose to go into Waterstones to find a single copy of, and pay full price for, a book they have never heard of by some unknown author, rather than getting a book they have heard of which is half price at the front of the store. In many ways, the market forces have pushed out young authors almost completely. And because now we only have Waterstones on the high street, if they don't choose to stock young authors then nobody will stock them - except perhaps an independent bookshop, but there are so few of them.'

As we move on to the subject of readership, her optimism returns. 'Books find their own readers, whoever those readers are supposed to be. My readers follow me in all sorts of directions without protesting that my books are not new versions of *Chocolat*. With my books, I would not presume to predict who the readers are going to be because I would get it wrong half the time, in the same way that the sales department gets it wrong half the time.' To illustrate this last point, Harris notes that 'sales departments still live under the delusion that women like to read about women' – a misconception proved wrong by Ian Rankin, who told her that his readership was predominantly female despite the fact that he writes quite masculine books. 'So where does that leave the marketing people?' she asks rhetorically.

It was also Ian Rankin who once advised Harris, 'Writing's easy. It's the author s**t that's hard.' She explains, 'People give you a lot of advice about failure, but nobody gives you advice about success. You are warned that it is terribly difficult to break into writing and to brace yourself for failure. Nobody tells you to brace yourself for success. It is just as difficult to become successful.'

'It is a bit like getting cancer in that people around you do not know how to cope with it. They will be unable to process the fact that you are not quite what they thought you were. There is a perception that you are going to change. Authors are often shy and retiring people; they will find it difficult to face the press. You need to be aware that you have to think twice about what you are going to say.' Harris concludes, 'be prepared for failure, but be prepared for success too, because both are equally traumatic.' ■

Joanne Harris' website contains a section devoted to tips on writing, finding agents and getting published, http://www.joanne-harris.co.uk/

Lee Child

NOVELS

- Untitled (Fall 2010)
- 61 Hours (Spring 2010)
- Gone Tomorrow (2009)
- Nothing To Lose (2008)
- Bad Luck and Trouble (2007)
- The Hard Way (2006)
- One Shot (2005)
- Persuader (2003)
- The Enemy (2004)
- Without Fail (2002)
- Echo Burning (2001)
- The Visitor (2000)
- Tripwire (1999)
- Die Trying (1998)
- Killing Floor (1997)

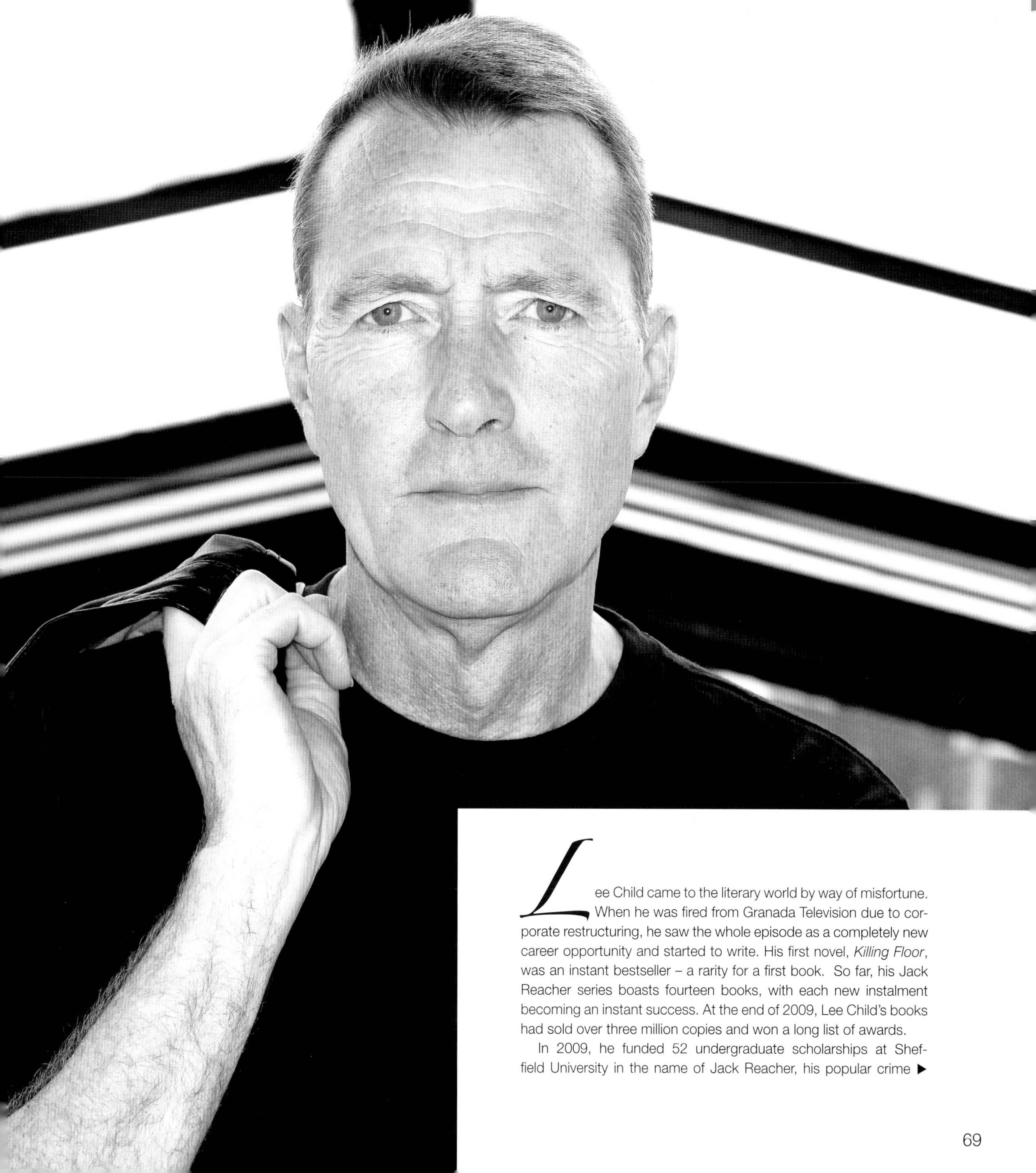

Lee Child came to the literary world by way of misfortune. When he was fired from Granada Television due to corporate restructuring, he saw the whole episode as a completely new career opportunity and started to write. His first novel, *Killing Floor*, was an instant bestseller – a rarity for a first book. So far, his Jack Reacher series boasts fourteen books, with each new instalment becoming an instant success. At the end of 2009, Lee Child's books had sold over three million copies and won a long list of awards.

In 2009, he funded 52 undergraduate scholarships at Sheffield University in the name of Jack Reacher, his popular crime ▶

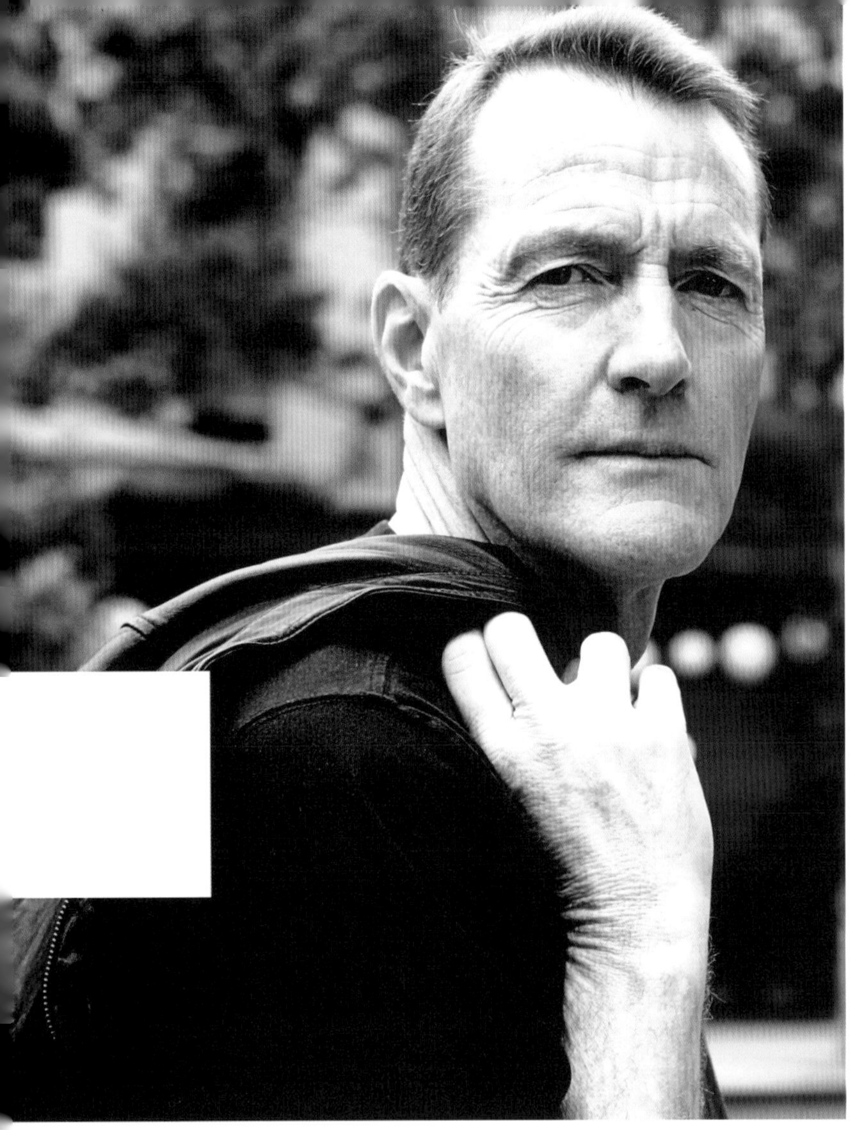

fighting hero.

Although I had never met Lee Child, I had spent hours in the company of Jack Reacher. So when the author appeared on the Radio 4 programme Saturday Live, I dropped everything to email the Radio 4 team in the vague hope that they will pass the message on.

A reply came almost instantaneously. Yes, Lee would take part, but he was on his way to catch a flight to Australia. That meant only one thing... I was about to have an e-conversation with one of the top 50 best-selling authors of this decade.

I read somewhere you start a novel with a climax in mind, and try to write towards that. How do you build the plot? Where does your inspiration come from?

The inspiration comes from whatever is on my mind at the time. It could be something I've read about, or heard about. Usually it suggests a scene or a situation or a revelation – or maybe just a crucial line of dialogue – and I keep that in mind as an eventual target. The plot kind of builds itself as a result of that process.

How do you create a protagonist for a character-based series? When you wrote Killing Floor, did you have a mental picture of what Reacher would be like five or ten or fifteen books later?

Good question. I don't think you can afford to think ahead too much. If you don't put 100% of everything into the first book, there won't be a fifth or a tenth or a fifteenth book, because the first one will fail. So I write them one at a time with no real plan for the future. And I'm not sure that series characters should change or develop very much. Readers like series because they're to some extent predictable and familiar and comforting.

Why did you make Jack Reacher a drifter and a loner? Was it because you didn't want to be boxed in?

Exactly. I was very aware that having a location- or employment-based series could get very restrictive later.

As a reader, what is your favourite genre?

I read most things, and enjoy most of them too, but I suppose my favourite is current events, or recent history – anything that explains things to me.

What was your biggest hurdle as a writer?

Accepting the truth that – barring miracles - it can take ten years to really get anywhere.

Is there a difference between the British public and the American public?

In terms of tastes and reactions, not really. In terms of readers taking chances with new writers, I think Americans are more adventurous.

All your titles have been sold to the movies. Do you write differently now that you know your stories might end up on the silver screen?

No, partly because Hollywood bought the series very early, so there wasn't really a before/after factor, and partly because if you change your vision as a result of external factors, then the books won't ring true.

What gave you the idea for the Jack Reacher scholarships?

I heard that good students were being forced to drop out of college due to financial pressures, and just like Reacher, I help where can.

What do you think made you a successful writer?

A: I think just showing up year after year with a good, solid book was 95% of the battle.

Do you have a method when you write?

I start at the beginning and keep going to the end – all linear, as much every day as I can.

What would you advise young writers to do? And not to do?

My advice is: don't listen to advice. A book needs to be vivid and organic, and it has to be the product of one mind alone – not a committee decision based on weighing other people's advice. Just do it. ■

To read more about Lee Child and his novels visit: www.leechild.com

Paul Hoffman

WORKS

- The Left Hand of God (2010)
- The Golden Age of Censorship (2007)
- The Wisdom of Crocodiles (2000)

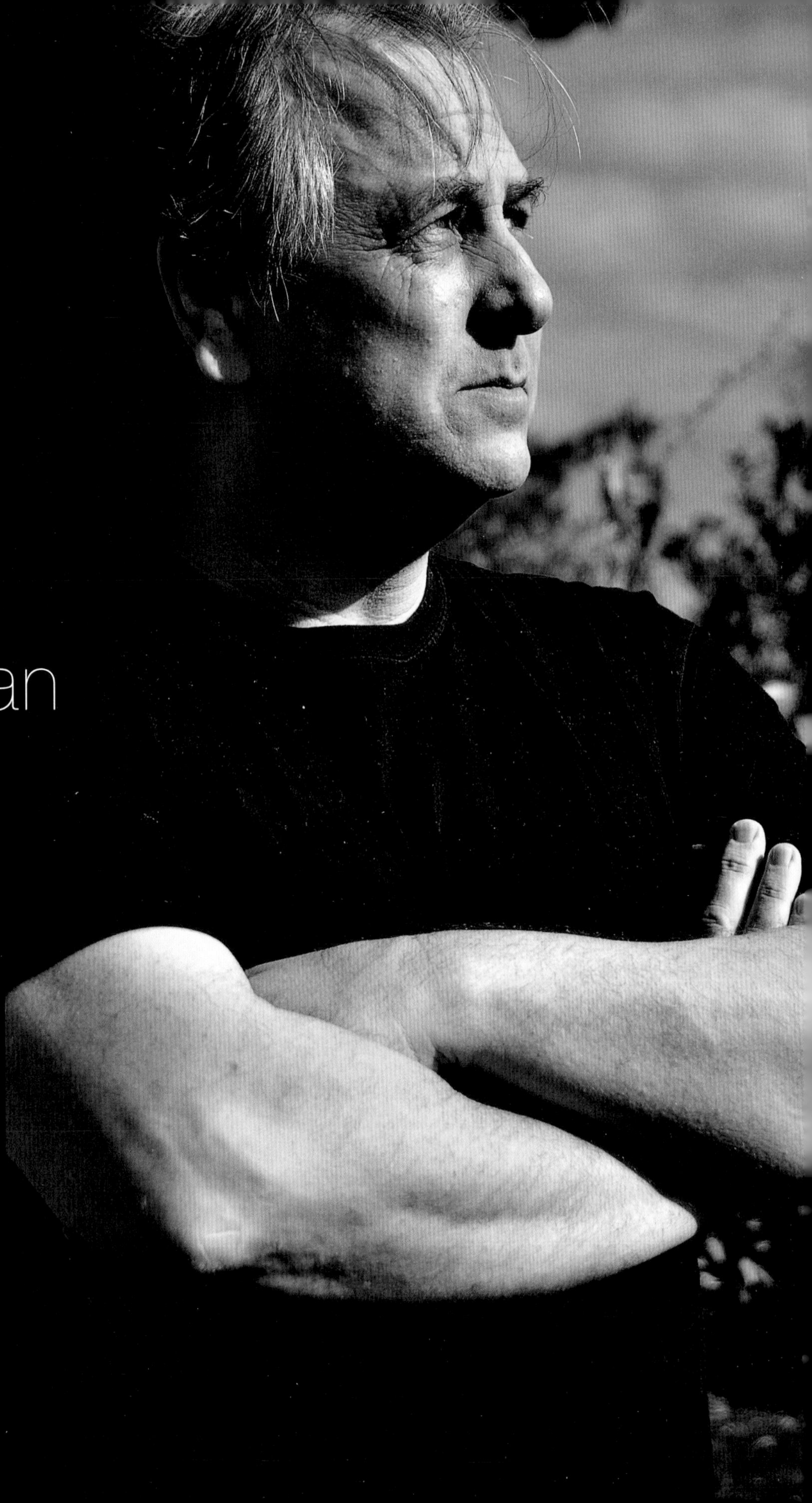

A mystical, fairytale childhood sounds idyllic to most, but not when that fairytale is written by sadistic monks and feral boys. Shut up for seven years in a Catholic boarding school ruled by 'thuggish' priests and boys who would have intimidated even the most hardened William Golding creations, Paul Hoffman sought refuge in his head. 'It wasn't just that it was violent,' he says. 'But almost everything that was interesting or valuable to human beings was stripped out of the place. You were never alone, you were always cold, always hungry – it was a prison.'

To escape their boredom the boys took various extreme ways out, from making their own drugs in the chemistry lab to strangling each other to the point of asphyxiation while chasing a huge high. Hoffman simply spent most of his time 'utterly removed,' dreaming up epic novels starring himself, with a supporting cast of adoring girls and monstrous baddies.

In real life, however, he found himself trapped in a dangerous world. The boys, who were invariably the 'hard-case' sons of army NCOs (as Hoffman was) or else plucked from the notorious Blackbird Lees council estate, grew up in a strange world of violence and intrigue. However, Hoffman turned the situation to his advantage, exercising his imagination and, without realising it, laying the foundations for his writing career. He recommends would-be authors to do the same. 'You can turn everything that comes your way into what you want to do,' he says. 'You have to be creatively like Shakespeare in that way – if you're not, if you're a Milton, it's going to be hard.'

Thankfully, the school closed when Hoffman was sixteen and reopened immediately as a mixed school. Hoffman had gone into the school as a dreamy little boy, but had come out as 'Dirty Harry with no qualifications.' This tough shell helped Hoffman forge his career. 'You have to be pathologically tough,' he says. 'A writer shouldn't be too precious about what story they do, they can always make it say what they want to say. But realise how tough it is, everyone is out there to kill your ideas, don't be such a twerp as to let them do it!'

Luckily, a teacher spotted his potential. She encouraged him to try for university and, due to his lack of qualifications, he applied to Oxford because they chose their students solely on entrance exam results.

Everyone but Hoffman and his teacher considered the idea pure fantasy. 'I was totally indifferent to what anyone thought,' he says. 'It seemed perfectly logical to me, so I just went and did it and got in and thought they were lucky to have me.'

Hoffman's Oxford years were particularly useful when writing *The Left Hand of God* because they played into his fairytale youth perfectly. As a lonely child he was surrounded by wicked wizards and monsters, terribly violent and cruel people and a father who fell from the sky - Hoffman's father was a pioneer of free-fall parachuting - before finding himself elevated to a princely new world. After leaving Oxford, he worked 'about twenty different jobs' as a messenger boy in the city, in a betting shop, labouring and teaching (which he did for

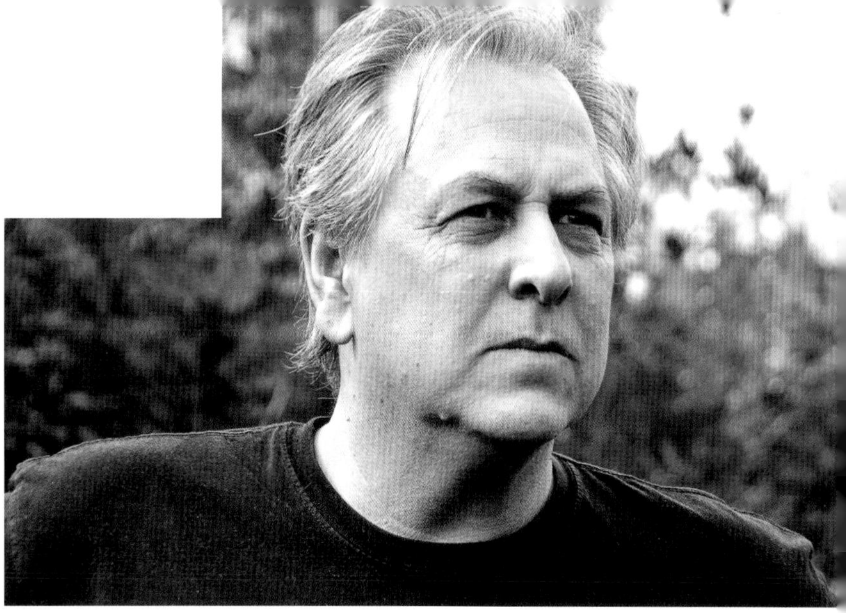

seven years) before eventually settling into a career as a film censor.

It was around this time that he began to write his first novel, The Wisdom of Crocodiles, which was turned into a film starring Jude Law before the book was even finished. Despite this, publisher after publisher rejected the book, until Hoffman realised he had to cut his thirteen-year, 300,000-word masterpiece into something more manageable. He tore through the book, slashing and burning six years worth of work until it was a more readable 180,000 words. But still no one was interested.

His agent was furious about no one publishing the book and decided to publish it himself - 'not something you should expect from your agent!' warns Hoffman. After three months of absolute silence, a glowing review in the Telegraph caught the eye of someone at Transworld, who eventually bought the manuscript. Hoffman had nearly finished writing *The Left Hand of God when his second book, The Golden Age of Censorship*, was published. But by then Transworld had 'had enough,' he says. 'They weren't making enough money from me.' So he began to look for a new publisher.

For six months his agent sent out the manuscript and for six months every response was the same - 'it's just not commercial' - until one day someone decided it was and suddenly everyone wanted it. Within a few weeks, *The Golden Age of Censorship* had sold in countries all over the world, and to date the book has been translated into 27 languages. 'For a few weeks they just kept calling me up and basically paying my mortgage,' Hoffman recalls. 'It does happen. But I'd like to stick together all the rejection letters - there are 10, 20 or 40 of these for every success. It can be a pretty hideous life.'

Hoffman finds a writer's life to be one of mixed blessings. "It's a wonderful experience to know that every day I can just go and do anything I want; it's just play. But the price can be pretty heavy. I came very close to not getting published and you're always going to be treading that line.' Still, he has once piece of sure-fire advice for every would-be author: 'Don't do it the way I did it. Don't write long books to start with; leave that until the end. Write a short one with lots of killing and sex.' ■

Philip Hoare

WORKS

- Leviathan (2008, first published 1995)
- England's Lost Eden: Adventures in a Victorian Utopia (2005)
- Spike Island: The Memory of a Military Hospital (2001)
- Wilde's Last Stand: Decadency, Conspiracy and the First World War (1997)
- Noel Coward: A Biography (1995)
- Serious Pleasures: The Life of Stephen Tennant (1990)

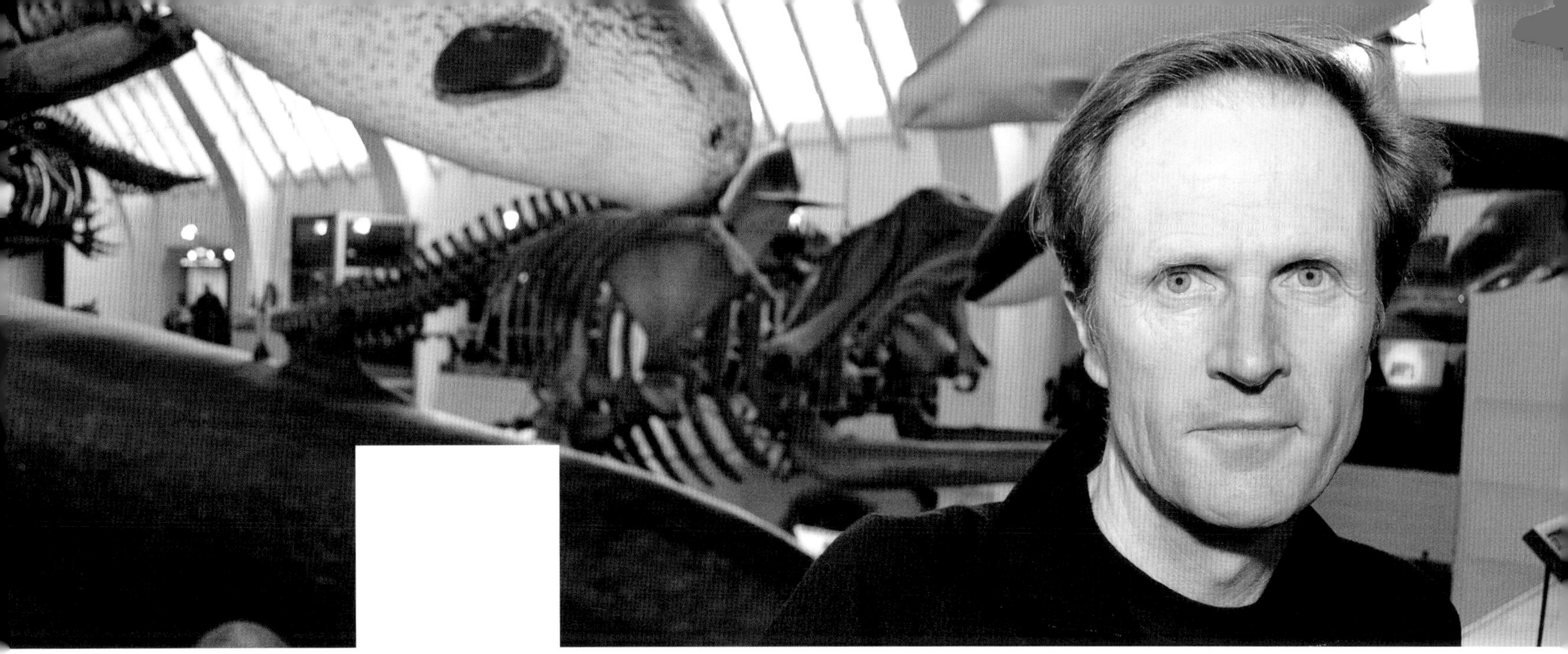

I meet Philip Hoare in the whale room at the Natural History Museum – it's packed and I have a hard time keeping up with him as he weaves his way through the crowd, skipping around baby buggies and oblivious tourists. I soon learn that Hoare applies this same enthusiasm and sprightly verve to each of his novels.

That's not to say they aren't a product of hard work (his writing schedule is punishing to the point of perversity and he devotes around 5 years to each book) but rather that he's so enthusiastic that the words jump eagerly toward the reader, just as if Hoare himself were reading them out in his breathless voice.

'If you write in a very world-weary, bored way, you're going to write boring books,' he says. 'It's my job as a writer to go and see these things, and convey that excitement to other people.' In many ways, he still sees the world through the eyes of a child. 'You have to maintain that sense of innocence, otherwise you become hardened to things and you stop seeing the magic.'

As a child, Hoare lost himself in the histories of Southampton and his school; the latter was the former home of Jane Austen and hid secret tunnels leading out to the sea. His college was no less inspiring, as it was Strawberry Hill, the fantastical gothic structure once inhabited by Horace Walpole. 'It was an amazing place,' Hoare recalls. 'It felt haunted and really stoked my romantic historical notions.'

This sense of specific place in a specific time is a recurring theme throughout Hoare's work. Just as the moors take on a character of their own in *Wuthering Heights* (Hoare's favourite novel), so too do the places featured in his books. As an author, Hoare takes on the role of Wuthering Heights' Nelly Dean: listening, watching, conveying. 'I'm just a conduit between the experience and the readers,' he explains. 'I'm always looking in; I'm never part of the action – that's generally how I feel about my life. And for me that's a good thing.'

At first glance there may not seem much to link his most recent book, *Leviathan*, to the rest of his work, but he brings the same passion to the topic of whales as he did to the obscure Edwardian aesthete Stephen Tennant. All his work is marked by obsession, and the slightest thing – a chance meeting, a mention in a book – can spark an obsession strong enough to fuel five years of research and writing.

Indeed, it is the thought of being without a subject (perhaps 'passion' is a better word) that most frightens Hoare. 'Waiting for it to come is a really painful process,' he admits. 'The very first time you open your newly published book, terror strikes you, because you've got to do another one! And what the hell's it going to be? And you flounder around, sometimes for months. Then you discover it's been there all along and it just needed time to develop.'

Has Hoare's love affair with whales ended since the writing of *Leviathan*? His friend, American film director John Waters, jokes that Hoare is so into whales he's a little bit sexually attracted to them, and writing just one book on the subject does not seem to have excised them from his imagination quite yet (he is currently working on another whale book but the details are strictly hush hush).

Hoare's parting words to me, enthusiastic as ever, are more of a plea than a farewell. 'You have to remember that the best thing about writing is writing. It's not having the book published, or the launch party. It isn't the reviews. It's writing the book and if you don't enjoy that then forget it, give up now. If you don't long to sit down and write, when you wake up in the morning and the first thing you want to do isn't write your book, give it up. It isn't important enough for you.' ■

Find out more at www.philiphoare.co.uk

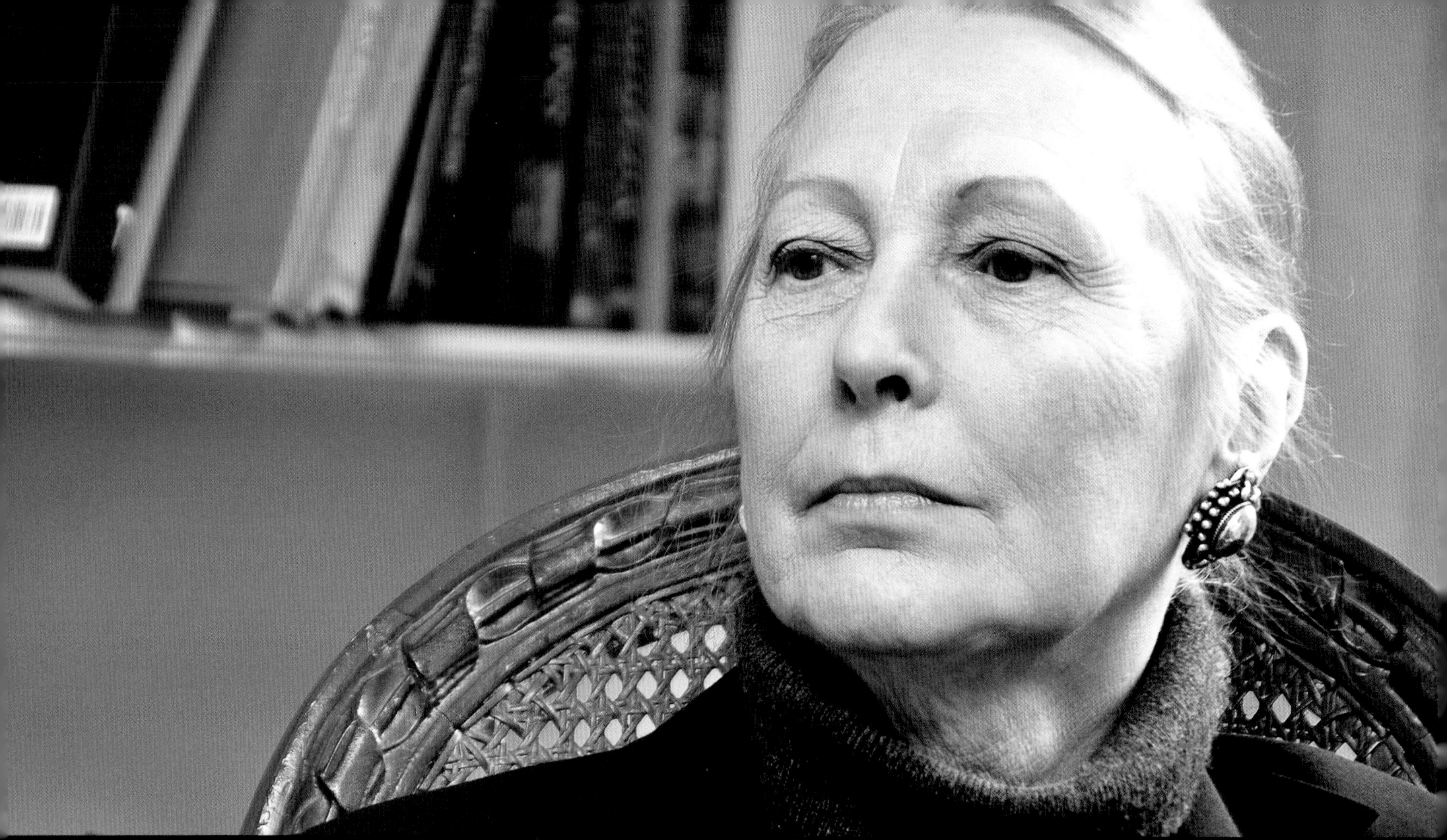

Sarah Bradford

WORKS

- Diana (2006)
- Lucrezia Borgia: Life, Love and Death in Renaissance Italy (2004)
- America's Queen: The Life of Jacqueline Kennedy Onassis (2000)
- Elizabeth: A Biography Of Her Majesty The Queen (1996)
- Splendours & Miseries: The Life of Sacheverell Sitwell (1993),
- George VI (1989)
- Disraeli (1982)
- Princess Grace (1984),
- Cesare Borgia: His Life and Times (1976)

As a child, gazing from the window of a speeding train, Sarah Bradford would dream that she was galloping on horseback with Rupert of the Rhine, jumping the hedges as she flew across the Somerset countryside. She was on her way to stay with cousins, who lived in a grand old pile, stuffed with huge portraits of illustrious ancestors in front of which the young Bradford would stand and stare, wondering who they were and how they lived.

'I think I was always interested in history and characters in history,' Bradford recalls. 'It's always been there with me – people in history, people in their time.' It was this passion that led her to write several decades' worth of bestselling biographies.

However, Bradford's dream was not to be a writer, but to study history at Oxford University, which she did after winning a college scholarship. At the time, places for women were scarce. 'I suppose I must have been quite clever,' she shrugs. And although she left to get married before completing her degree ('Can you imagine how barking?' she says. 'There was the most awful row!'), she credits her university education with bestowing upon her the research skills that became key to her career.

While Bradford agrees that not everyone needs a university education to become a writer, she feels it set her on her way. 'You're not spoonfed,' she says. 'That was a great change from school; you have to learn how to work on your own for great periods and they expect high standards from you. It set me up in very good stead for my own research. And that's something I will always be grateful for.'

Despite a growing urge to write, Bradford had no idea how to go about getting published. 'It was a very different era then and that's why I think I started late,' she says. 'Unless you were born into a literary family, if you were a normal, middle-class sort of girl, you wouldn't even think about it.' So she travelled the world with her husband, living in idyllic locales such as Barbados, Portugal and Sardinia, where it wasn't possible to carry out research.

During this period, she briefly focused on fiction writing, producing a 'very silly story' which she hoped would be serialised in a woman's magazine, although nothing came of it. Bradford labels it her 'only real failure so far,' probably because her heart wasn't in the project. 'It was all the archives, documents and other people's lives that fascinated me,' she admits. 'Not this.'

Despite this initial setback, Bradford carried on and collaborated with a friend on a guide to Portugal, which won her an agent. 'I didn't know any agents then, so I sent the manuscript around, as you do,' she says. 'I got a very nice agent called Juliet O'Hay, who was one of the greats, and through her I was commissioned to do a book on port, of which I knew nothing!'

With the encouragement of the great George Weidenfeld, she then wrote a biography of Cesare Borgia, which was turned into a beautiful but ultimately unsuccessful bodice-ripping BBC television series, and from there her career began to soar. A book on Disraeli followed and, in order to finance it, Bradford worked for the famous tailor Hayward of Mount Street, where 'not much work went on' beyond 'ripping up suits, answering telephones and getting flirted with' by the likes of Terence Stamp and David Bailey.

Researching Disraeli while working part-time and bringing up children was hard work. 'I don't know how I did it,' Bradford says. 'Of course, the younger you are, the more energy you have, and of course being terribly interested in what you do always helps.' By the time she started George IV she was working in the manuscripts department of Christie's, 'which was wonderful,' she says, 'although I had no idea what I was doing.' Because she was working part-time, the book took six years to complete. 'Normally,' she advises, 'if you're devoting all your time to it and you don't have to do other jobs, three years should be long enough.'

Bradford recommends that, although concentration and hard work are important, writers need to follow their passions. 'Some books I have had to do because I was asked to – *Diana* being one of those. Huge sums were dangled under my nose,' she reveals. 'But Jackie Kennedy and Disraeli were both my ideas, and I think it works best when they're your idea. If you're bored from the start there's really no point in doing it, is there?'

However, Bradford acknowledges that achieving commercial success can be difficult for non-fiction writers nowadays. 'I was quite lucky to get into that world when I did,' she says. 'When I wrote about Jackie [Kennedy Onassis] there were very big sales, but not so much now. It's not fashionable. People are less interested in history, less well-educated than they were and I think biography has suffered as a result of that. It's a great way of learning history - it's all the most exciting bits!'

Since the publication of her last book in 2007, Bradford has spent much of her time writing articles and book reviews but, she warns, 'it's not the same as doing a book.' Now she's making up for that by working on two books at once: one on Queen Victoria and the other on Queen Elizabeth II. 'I've missed it terribly,' she says, 'because I think it's part of your identity - being a writer.' And in one shrewd question she gets to the heart of the matter: 'If you're not actually working on a book, what are you doing?' ■

Find out more at www.sarahbradford.co.uk.

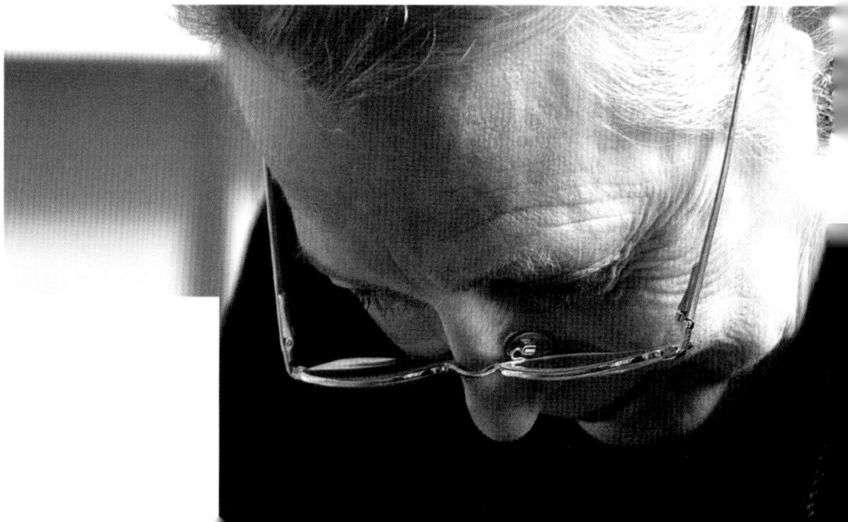

Simon Mawer

WORKS

- The Glass Room(2009)
- Swimming to Ithaca (2006)
- The Fall (2003)
- The Gospel of Judas (2000)
- A Jealous God (1996)
- The Bitter Cross (1992)
- A Place in Italy (1992)
- Chimera (1989)

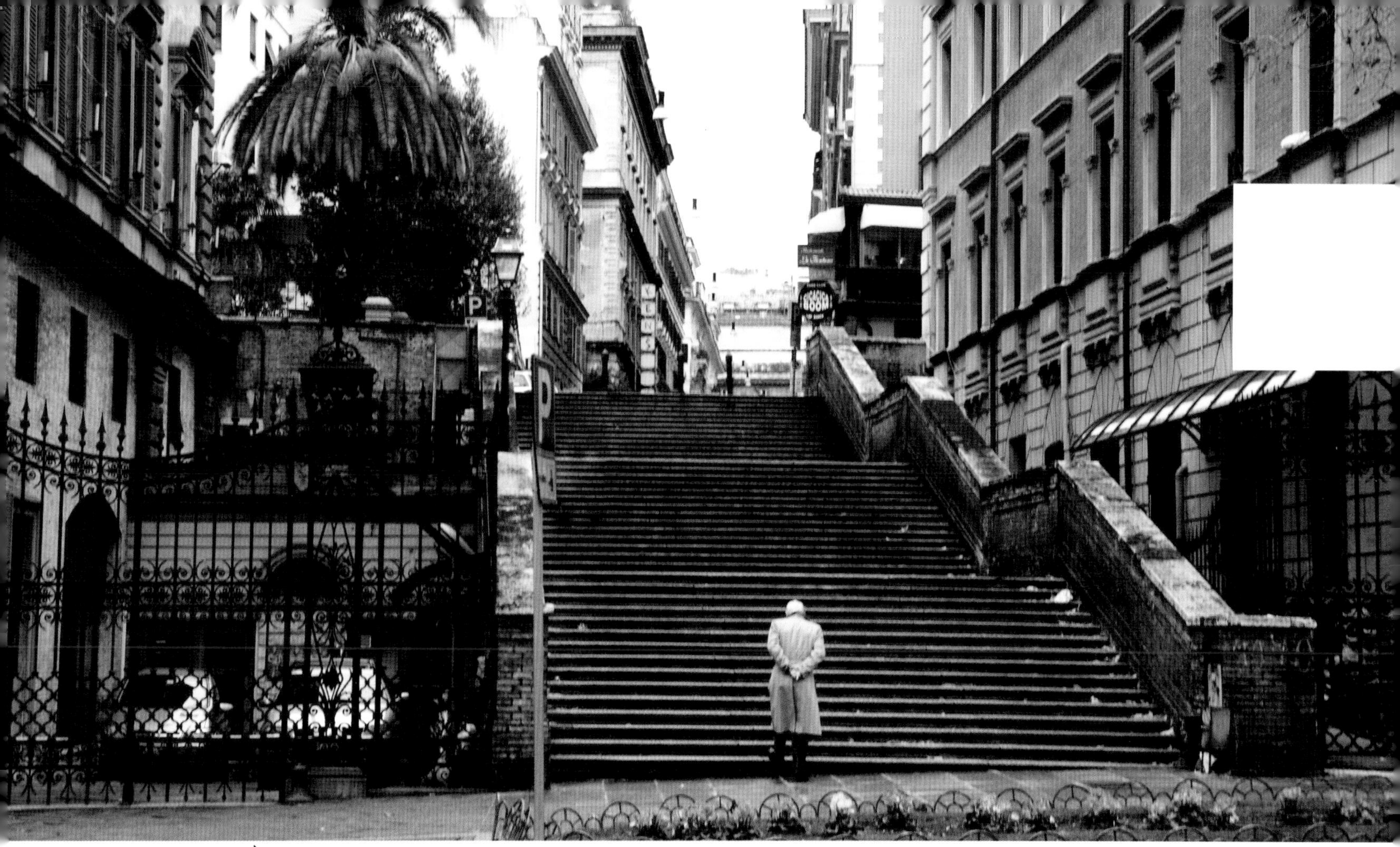

The Glass Room was shortlisted for the Booker Prize in 2009 and it was also shortlisted for the Walter Scott Prize for Historical Fiction, so it was extremely fortunate to have been able to get an interview with Simon Mawer even if we were miles apart.

Were you a creative child? Did you write?

I guess I wrote a bit – I've got a trunk in the basement full of mouldering juvenilia – but I was also very lazy and so not a lot got done. But I talked. I used to regale schoolmates with lurid tales of death and sex and war. And I did create fantasy worlds in my mind, some of which have appeared, albeit in much-altered forms, in my books.

How did you find school?

My father was in the RAF so I was at boarding school from the age of eight, as my parents moved around all the time. I hated it until the age of fifteen, when I moved to a mixed boarding school and discovered girls. From then on I loved it. The trouble with boarding school is a brutal lack of privacy. However, that does bring advantages for a budding author as it forces you to create an inner world that is separate from the loud, rackety, impersonal world all around. That isn't to say I was a particularly introverted or solitary person. I had the usual clutch of friends and played the usual sports and all those kinds of things. But there was an inner me that watched and thought.

Did you continue to write creatively at university?

No. I did almost nothing at university beyond enjoying myself in a very low-key way. I did a bit of acting – I was potentially quite a good actor – but not much else. Certainly very little academic work. That's probably the part I regret most now. I love biology, which was my subject. I find the ideas of biology eternally fascinating and relevant.

Tell me about the events that led you to write your first book.

My first completed book – which, after being entirely rewritten, became my second published novel – was a historical novel centred on the Knights of St John in the 16th century. I was living in Malta at the time and was fascinated by the palaces and fortifications of the Knights on the island. It seemed a good subject for a novel and I spent hours in the Royal Malta Library reading an 18th-century Italian history of the Knights. My first published novel, *Chimera*, came out of a walking expedition I took through the countryside of Alto Lazio with a group of students. Upper Lazio is real Etruscan country, and was probably more densely populated then than it is now. One day we came across an Etruscan archaeological site (excavated ▶

by the Swedish School at Rome in the 1960s) situated beside an abandoned railway station. There was no road connection to anywhere – just this abandoned railway line passing the station and continuing onto a steel girder bridge across a wide river valley. The whole railway station/line/bridge is itself a kind of archaeological relic and the juxtaposition of the two – railway and Etruscan town – seemed so startling that it fired my imagination. How to link the two together? That's *Chimera*, and a damn good book it is too!

What was the writing process like for your first book?

If we consider *Chimera* to be my first book, I wrote it longhand over a two-year period, I guess. I then typed it up and sent it off to some publishers, knowing that it wasn't good enough, but I was fed up with writing it. They all said no thank you, as I knew they would. So I took it back, added a whole new dimension to the book which increased it by about a third, and sent it out again, this time to three major agents. The rewrite took about another eighteen months. The first agency didn't even want to read it, but the second agency wrote me a long letter explaining exactly why they felt they couldn't take it on. That was the moment that I realised it was marketable, because they had spent so much time with it and wrote such a considered reply. My third shot was accepted and I've been with the same agent ever since.

How long does it take you to write now?

It takes me slightly less time to write a novel now because - I hope - I'm experienced enough to get the measure of the book at the start. Having said that, it still takes eighteen months or so to write a book and I'm still afraid of what I'm writing not being good enough.

How do you deal with rejection or disappointment?

I haven't really been rejected, except for the first version of Chimera, which I knew at the time wasn't good enough. The second version was sold on first submission to Hamish Hamilton. But the way to accept rejection or disappointment is this: if you know damn well it is justified, then get down to putting the thing right. If it really isn't justified – but that's the catch! – then ignore it. The difficulty is not being able to recognise when your own work just isn't good enough. It's not a problem I suffer from!

Has it ever been so tough that you considered giving it all up and doing a 'normal' job?

I've always had a 'normal' job. I have been a teacher all my adult life. But I've always thought of myself as primarily a writer because that is what I am. So I couldn't give it up.

Do you have any writing rituals or habits?

Just keep writing. And if I'm not writing, then I just sit there staring at the computer screen. Blackmail, really. I play a lot of Patience.

How do you deal with writers block?

I've no idea. Does it exist? Maybe it's what I have all the time when I'm not actually writing, which is most of the time. So how do I deal with it? See above.

What are the best and worst aspects of your job?

Writing is an awful, boring, solitary grind. So actually doing it is the worst aspect. The best aspect? Just having written. The second best? When someone who is disinterested - that includes my agent or publisher, even though they are interested parties, because they are professionals - says they think it's good.

Were you surprised at how much publicity and promotion you had to do yourself?

Not really. Because I live outside of Britain I fear that I did much less promotion in the early days than I should have. That's why, after seven rather high-quality novels, I was still described as a 'dark horse' when *The Glass Room* was shortlisted for the Man Booker Prize. Now things are different. If I can say this in a modest way, the world is beating a path to my door.

Do you read your reviews? How do you handle the bad ones?

I haven't had bad reviews. Or if I have, I've forgotten them. What makes you sit up and take notice is when, in the midst of a generally positive review, a reviewer makes a negative critical comment that you are in agreement with. It's worth taking notice of that.

You were nominated for the Man Booker Prize in 2009; what do literary prizes mean to you?

I've won other prizes and, beyond a moment's small sense of achievement, they have meant relatively little. But not winning the Booker is bigger than actually winning the lesser prizes and it has meant a very great deal. It has raised my profile enormously and boosted my sales. *The Glass Room* has sold very well for a piece of literary fiction, and is still selling over a year after its first publication. It'd be naïve of me to think that that would have happened purely on the merits of the book alone. Of course it was only on the shortlist through its merits!

Do you feel it's important to be around other creative people?

Not really. A novelist's life is far too turned in on itself to take any notice of people around you.

Finally, and most importantly, what is the most important piece of advice you could give to young writers?

Don't have any illusions. Writing novels is solitary and tedious. You have to write hundreds of thousands of words and it takes ages and then it isn't any good and you have to go back and start all over again. On top of all that, you almost certainly won't make enough money to support yourself, let alone a family. Take up-something fun, like being an accountant or a bank manager.

On the other hand, you know what the immortal David Hockney said? 'I've heard of many a bank manager who wanted to be a poet, but I've never heard of a poet who wanted to be a bank manager.' For 'poet,' you can substitute 'novelist.' ■

www.simonmawer.com

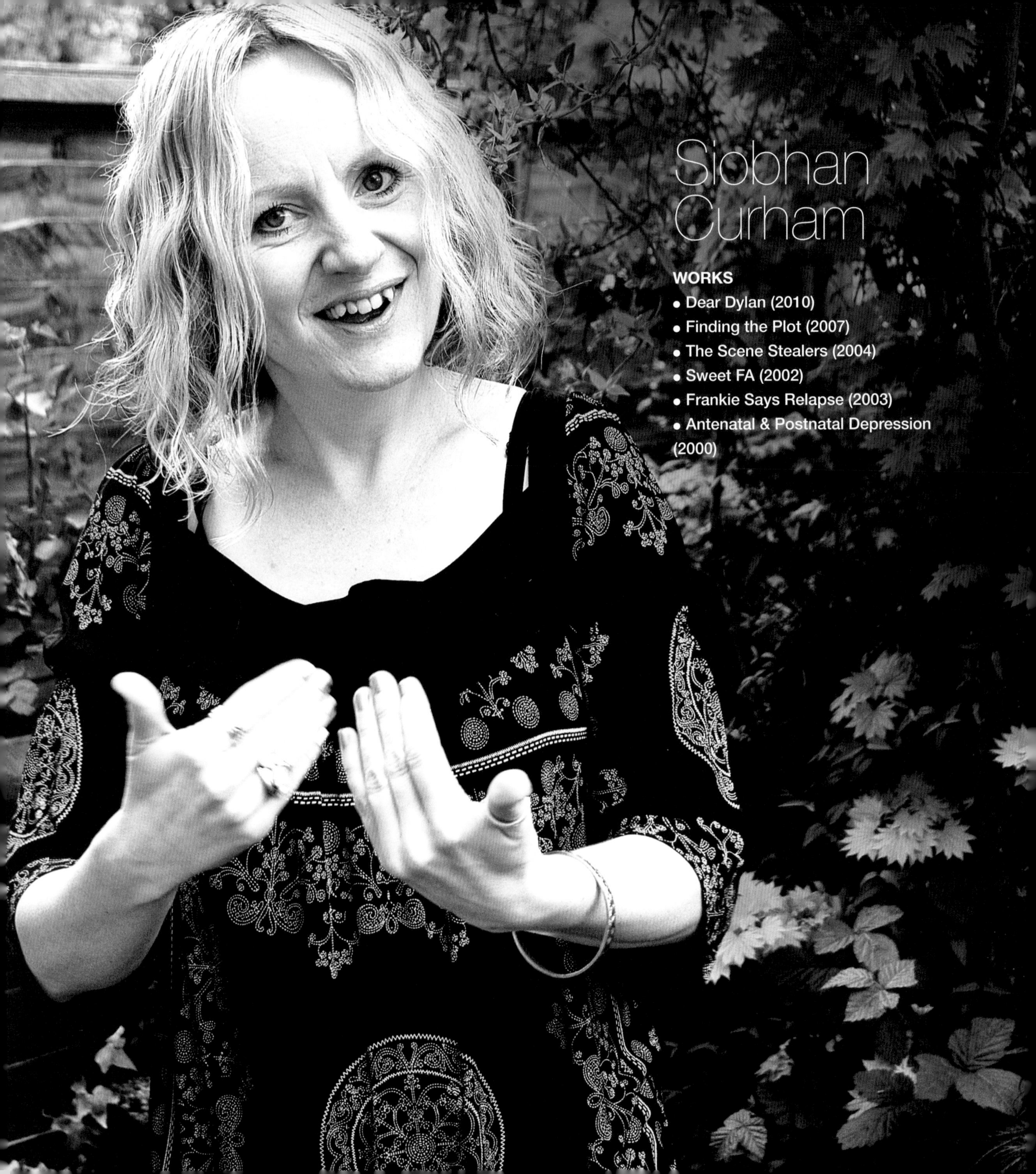

Siobhan Curham

WORKS

- Dear Dylan (2010)
- Finding the Plot (2007)
- The Scene Stealers (2004)
- Sweet FA (2002)
- Frankie Says Relapse (2003)
- Antenatal & Postnatal Depression (2000)

As a child, Siobhan Curham would visit the library on a Saturday morning and spend her weekend immersed in the magical worlds conjured up by her favourite authors. As an adult, however, despite releasing four well-received books in quick succession, Curham found herself increasingly disillusioned with the traditional publishing industry and went on to explore the world of self-publishing.

It wasn't until she fell pregnant with her son that Curham initially found the time to write. 'I had no contacts in the book world, so I thought I should start at the bottom of the ladder and work my way up,' she says. Mapping out a five-year plan to become a published author, Curham embarked on a correspondence course in freelance journalism. 'I figured if I could get some articles published and build a name that way, it would probably be easier to get published when I eventually wrote a book.'

After earning her press pass, which 'looked like it had been laminated in someone's garage,' Curham began sending out all manner of 'weird and wonderful' articles. 'I got a fair few rejections and there were times when I just thought, Why am I bothering?' But a week or two would go by and I'd get another idea for an article and get all excited again.'

Curham recommends that writers of both fiction and non-fiction find a subject that has never been written about before or to find a completely new angle on a previously covered subject. Following her own advice, the first article she had published was on the rarely-discussed phenomenon of antenatal depression, which proved so popular with readers that she decided to write a book on the topic.

'I put an appeal in a magazine saying I was looking for case studies,' Curham recalls. 'And an editor from Random House saw it and called me asking if they could publish the book. It was really thrilling, but of course I had to try to play it cool because you don't want to seem to eager.'

Buoyed by this reception, Curham decided to write her first novel. She would work while her son was asleep, tapping away on an old typewriter and photocopying her manuscript in the local co-op because she couldn't afford a computer.

'I had no idea what I was doing at all,' Curham admits. 'So I remember looking at other novels, not copying people, but seeing how you should do things - how much time you spend describing a room, for example.' She recommends going to writing groups and reading books on writing for guidance. 'There is one in particular that I always recommend to writers just starting out,' she says. 'It's called *Solutions for Novelists* by Sol Stein, an American editor who wrote the book from an editor's point of view, showing you what they're looking for in terms of structure. Once I read that I felt like I knew what I was doing.'

Once the book was finished, Curham picked a handful of agents from *The Writer's and Artist's Yearbook* and one of them signed her up straight away. 'Within a week I'd got a two-book deal from Hodder & Stoughton and a buyer for the film rights,' she remembers. 'It was just incredible. One minute I was standing in the village shop photocopying and the next minute I was going down to London to meet with film producers. It felt like a fairytale.'

Following on from that success, Curham published two more novels, but at the same time became disillusioned with the industry. 'It went from being a real high to being quite difficult,' she reveals. 'I thought if you had a book deal with a company the size of Hodder, you'd have a big marketing budget behind you but that's not the case. It's sink or swim; they'll take you on but they won't really invest that much money in you until you've built up a readership.' Increasingly worried, Curham would call her publisher's publicity department with ideas, only to be told they just didn't have the budget. 'It was frustrating and it did knock my confidence a lot, so after my third book with them, I was really dejected and I didn't know what to do.'

It was at this point that Curham stumbled upon an article about the new print-on-demand technology that was making it easier to self-publish. 'So I decided to give it a go,' she says, 'and I self-published my fourth novel in 2007.' Although she learned a lot from the experience, she realises in hindsight that she made some mistakes, such as editing the book herself (at one point her characters sit down to a 'moth-watering' meal). ▶

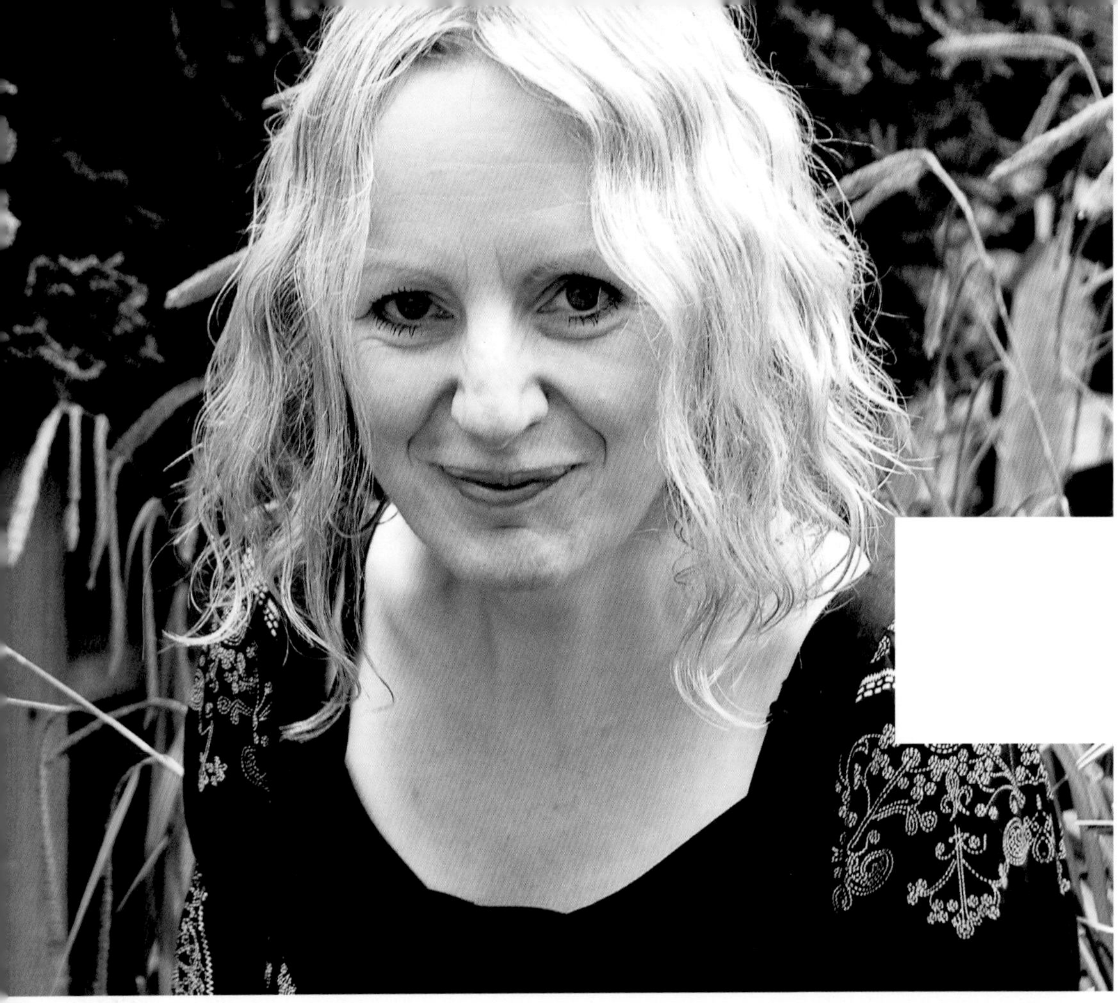

She encountered another problem when trying to get the book reviewed. 'All my other books had been published in the national press and I assumed that would stand me in good stead, but I didn't manage to get it reviewed anywhere,' Curham says. 'Having said that, with all the advances on the internet, it feels like getting reviews in national papers isn't quite so important anymore, because there are so many websites out there now.'

With her latest book, *Dear Dylan*, Curham was actually offered a two-book deal from a traditional publishing house, which she turned down, choosing to continue self-publishing instead. Despite being long-listed for the Young Minds Book Award, she hasn't bothered approaching the national papers for reviews, instead targeting websites run by and for teens. 'I guess in the online world and in the teen market there isn't the snobbery that traditional publishing still feels towards self-publishing,' she muses.

While Curham feels grateful to her publishers for taking a chance on her, she also feels the traditional publishing establishment is reaching a 'sink or swim' moment of its own. 'The old school can come across as being quite arrogant,' she observes. 'The publishers and the agents have this little cliquey world and it seems to me they're quite scared, because there are all these developments happening and the power is being taken away from them and they don't know what to do.'

It's precisely because of this change that 'it's a really exciting time to be a writer,' says Curham. Lots of independent publishers are springing up and collectives of writers are setting up their own companies thanks to new technology such as ebooks. 'And that's got to be a good thing,' she says, 'because the traditional publishing world has become so narrow – it's all celebrities and misery memoirs.' According to Curham, however, editors are also sick of seeing the same things pass across their desks. After she sent her *Dear Dylan* manuscript out, she received a call from a commissioning editor who said, 'It's so refreshing to get this because everything agents are sending is so stale, and if I read another book about wizards I'm going to scream!'

To ensure that yours is not the manuscript making that poor editor scream, Curham simply advises to write from the heart. 'Don't try to be commercial about it,' she says. 'By the time the book is published, it's two years down the line and trends have moved on. If you want your work to stand out, just write what you feel passionately about and don't be swayed by what you think is the next big thing because it will affect your writing. If you're writing something that means a lot to you, the writing will have a kind of energy about it and be alive with passion and enthusiasm. And who knows? You could be the one setting the next trend.' ■

www.siobhancurham.co.uk

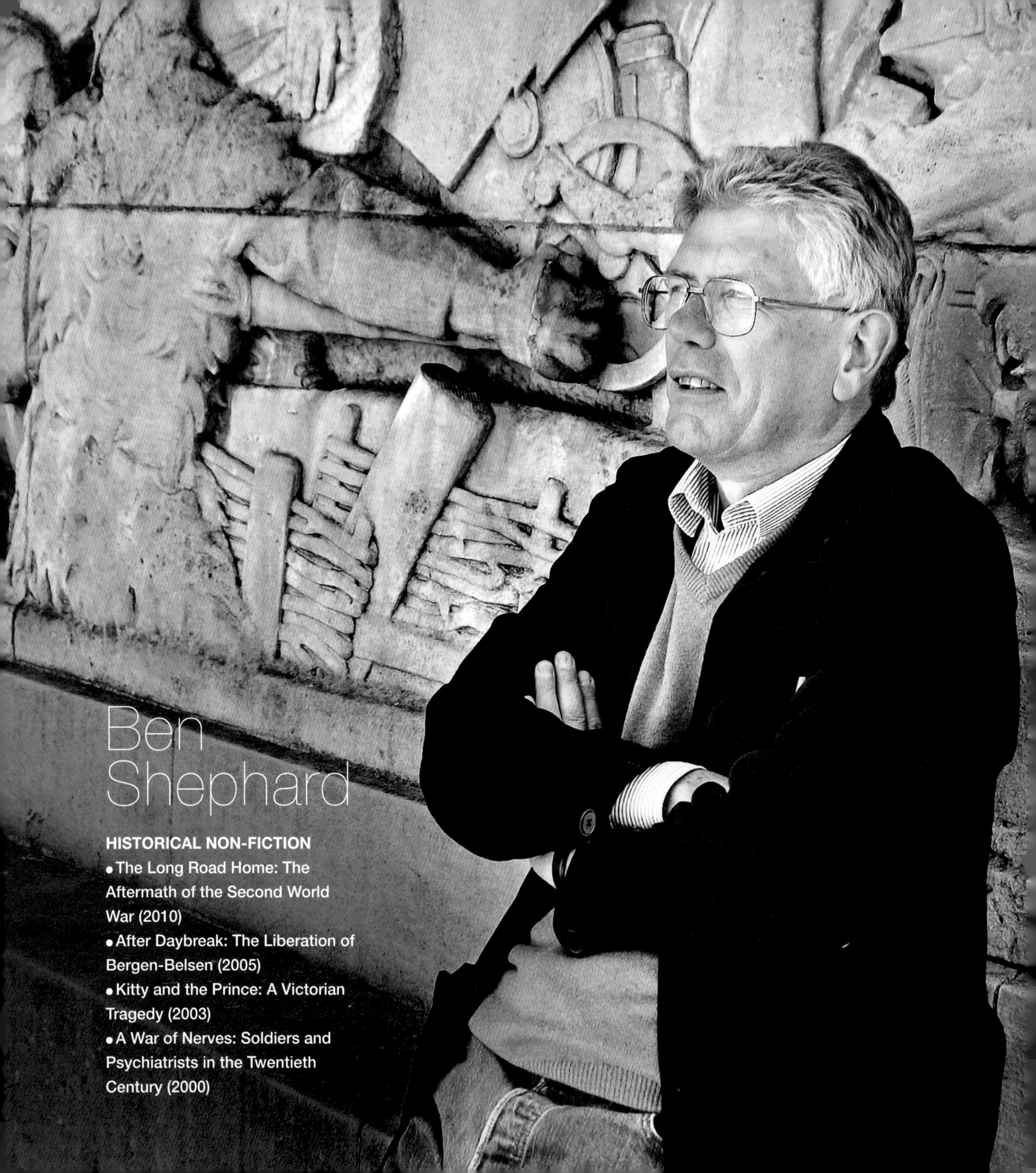

Ben Shephard

HISTORICAL NON-FICTION

- The Long Road Home: The Aftermath of the Second World War (2010)
- After Daybreak: The Liberation of Bergen-Belsen (2005)
- Kitty and the Prince: A Victorian Tragedy (2003)
- A War of Nerves: Soldiers and Psychiatrists in the Twentieth Century (2000)

Having been born and raised in South Africa just after the Second World War, Ben Shephard felt his British heritage keenly and quickly developed an interest in - and lifelong love of - British history.

Shephard's fascination with history and his ability to disseminate it was first stoked at Westminster School, where, he says, he was 'extraordinarily well-taught,' and then honed by a career in television. He credits his time working on the Emmy-winning The World at War television series with his ability to explain complex historical and political topics. 'In TV you have to explain British colonialism in a sentence, and that's really good training because it forces you to distil things to their essence,' he says. 'I was surrounded by extremely gifted television writers who would endlessly shape and reshape a sentence and rework the words until they fitted a picture exactly.'

However, he does not look back on his Oxford University days with any particular fondness. 'History was very badly taught in my college at that time,' he recalls. 'I have never drawn on it at all - they didn't give me any particular research skills .' He does feel, though, that the combination of going to Westminster and working on The World at War gave him a necessary 'kind of arrogant self-belief that everyone else has got it wrong and you've got it right. It also gives you a kind of sense that you don't give up when you can't immediately find what you're looking for.'

Shephard believes that 'there's a terrible superficiality in the way history is taught to undergraduates in this country,' although he does concede one benefit. 'Obviously you have to write essays, and that means that if you go on to be a writer, the concept of expressing yourself in print is not anathema.'

It was in 1989, after almost 20 years working in television, that Shephard first thought of writing a book. Browsing in a Boston bookshop one day, he was struck by how many books there were on the Vietnam War. 'They all had titles like Trauma and Transformation,' he recalls. 'They were part of a therapeutic literature, which had emerged from the Vietnam War and which propounded the idea of post-traumatic stress disorder [PTSD].' Having interviewed 150 World War II soldiers, Shephard believed that the modern psychiatric attitude to trauma was flawed, and he decided to prove it.

He spent the next ten years researching and writing his first book, *A War of Nerves: Soldiers and Psychiatrists in the Twentieth Century.* 'My advice to anyone is, for God's sake, don't go down my path. The trouble with this sort of book is that they take as long as they take and you can't rush it.' Shephard fully believes that a book must be released at exactly the right time – for him, this time was heralded by the publication of two other works questioning the validity of PTSD, which meant his book was much better received than it would have been five years earlier. 'There's a lot of waiting to feel as if you're ready to give birth,' he explains. 'You're slightly prolonging the pregnancy because you know it isn't quite the right time.'

To write the book Shephard had to get to grips with 20th century psychiatry, psychology and neurology, as well as a huge amount of military history. 'I'm incredibly undisciplined and ridiculously over-thorough,' he admits. 'I didn't write much, other than notes, for five or six years.' For Shephard, this was a quest in pursuit of an intellectual goal. 'I just wanted to understand this subject for myself,' he explains. 'My path is a very odd one and not one that anyone else would want to follow, because it is that of an obsessive. I could only follow it because my wife was the breadwinner, working as a Commissioning Editor at Channel Four'.

With no background in psychiatry, Shephard had to work at being taken seriously in that world. After a certain amount of research he began to give talks at conferences and publish articles in journals, which he considers 'very useful when you're not quite sure of your ground,' and it gave him 'street cred' which enabled him to take his research further, get research grants and visit psychiatric conferences abroad. Although *A War of Nerves* has been hailed as a 'masterpiece' by some, Shephard believes some of those early papers he gave were better than the final book. 'The material was fresher then,' he explains. 'When you're still in ▶

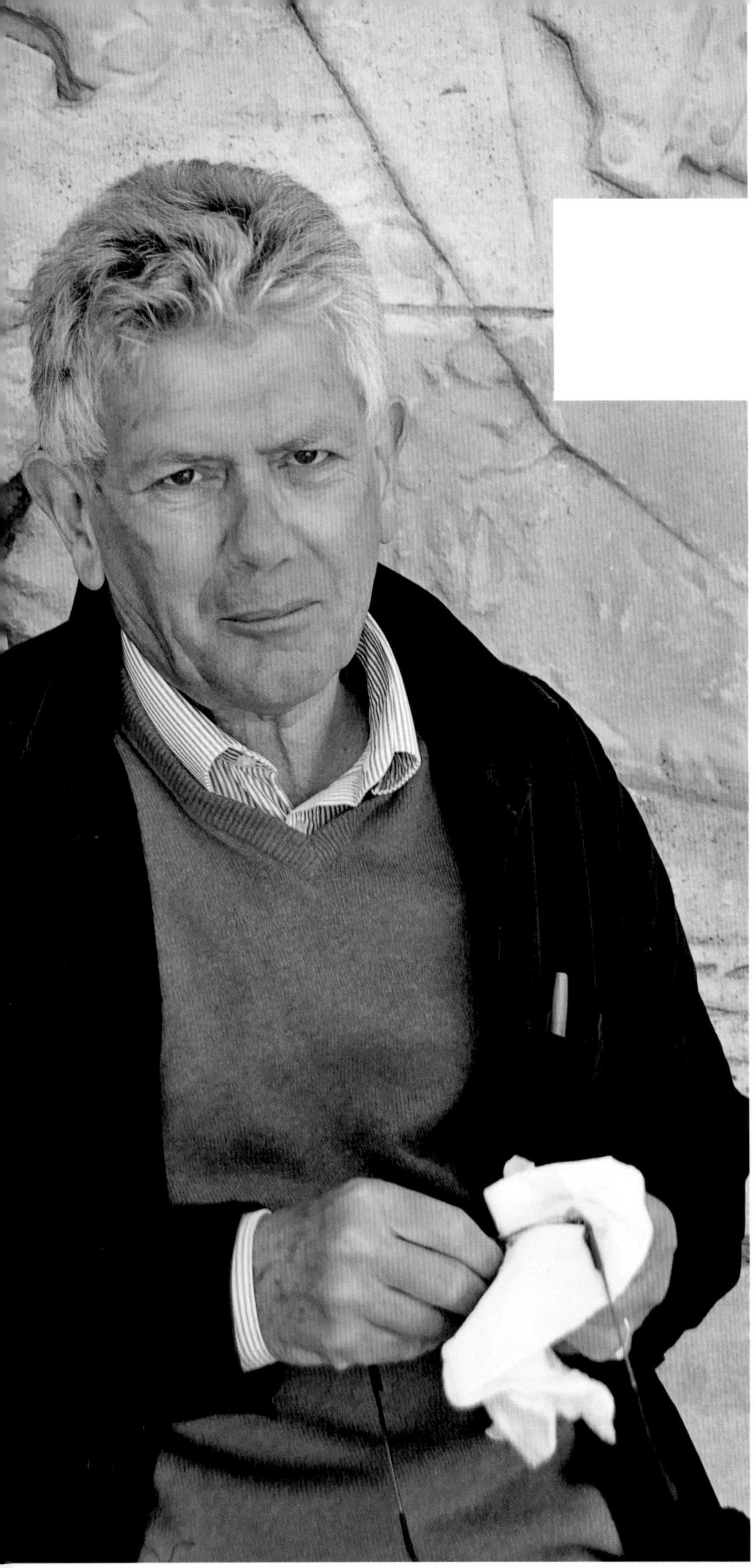

the process of discovery the material is labile; it's exciting and it's wonderful.'

The problem was stitching this material together to create a comprehensive but readable narrative. 'Ideally you want to make it flow, you want to have seamless prose,' Shephard explains. 'But at a certain stage it goes dead on you, like cement - it just sets. So I have to work elsewhere and then come back to it. Then I create a paragraph-by-paragraph model of what I've got, and then a new model of what I need. I think it's much more instinctive for fiction writers. For me it's like climbing the Eiger.'

A history writer has to create a fine balance between accuracy and entertainment. Shephard accomplishes this through the skilful use of anecdotes. 'That's where you find all sorts of fascinating bits of information,' he says. 'For example, during the Second World War there was a group of tank men in the desert who all dressed up as transvestites in between battles. Those are the sorts of things that need to be in that book - otherwise it's not human enough.'

Although A War of Nerves, which Shephard considers a 'necessary book,' made him an authority on the history of psychiatry, he often wonders what he has gained from the experience, since he remains 'unable to capitalise' on it. 'Because I don't have the academic standing or the commercial clout,' he explains, 'I just had to move on to become a jobbing writer.' Although Shephard's subsequent books have been well-received, he feels that they 'haven't been necessary in quite the same way.' However, he quickly adds, 'That isn't reflected in my work because I'm more professional than that. There is a difference in being mad and obsessive as I was with my first book and being a professional writer.'

Shephard often refers to himself as 'mad,' especially in career terms. 'A lot of people who try to write something worthwhile are mad,' he says. He believes you'd have to be mad to choose such a badly paid path. I got paid £6,500 for *A War of Nerves*, and I must have spent that much on photocopying and buying research books on Amazon over the ten years it took me to write.'

Ultimately, he feels that writing is 'a mug's game - there's no money in it. I get very bored and fed up because I feel I'm good at what I do and I don't get paid very much for doing it.' Even the upsides don't entirely outweigh this. 'The great compensation for the writer's life is finding stuff in archives, which is a wonderfully satisfying thing to do; nothing beats it. The trouble is that it's not enough. It's not enough to get praise in the newspapers. You want more than that, but,' he warns, 'you're not going to get more.' Despite this, he refuses to change his writing simply for the sake of commercial success. 'My agent says, "If you stick the word 'squadron' in the title I can get you another £10,000," but I just can't do that. I write books,' he says simply, 'because I want to know about things.' ■

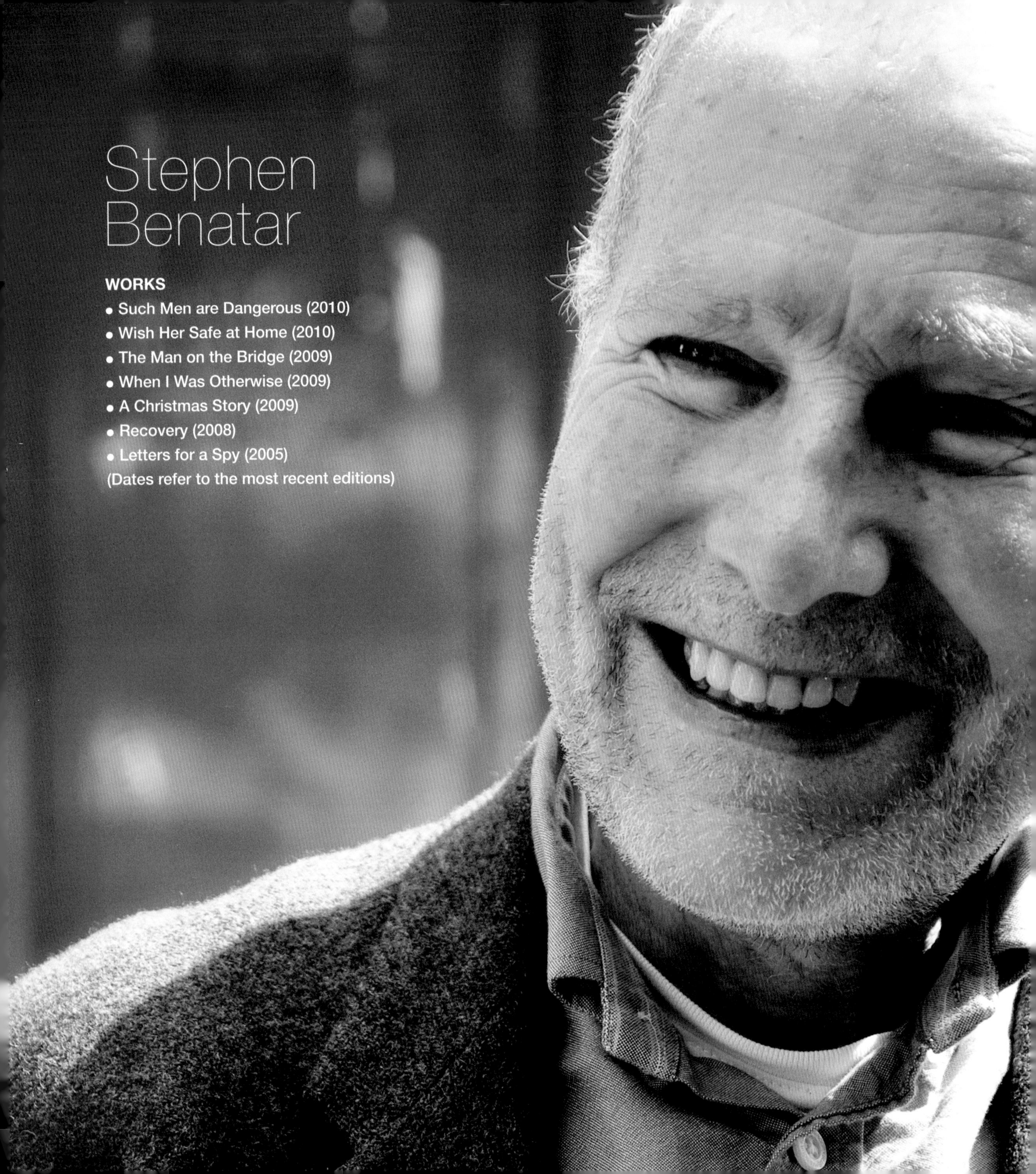

Stephen Benatar

WORKS

- Such Men are Dangerous (2010)
- Wish Her Safe at Home (2010)
- The Man on the Bridge (2009)
- When I Was Otherwise (2009)
- A Christmas Story (2009)
- Recovery (2008)
- Letters for a Spy (2005)

(Dates refer to the most recent editions)

If a soft-spoken, well-dressed man approaches you in a bookshop this weekend, don't shy away - there's a good chance it's Stephen Benatar. He will more than likely slip a copy of his book Wish Her Safe At Home into your hands, with a quiet 'Would you be so kind?' and melt into the background once more, leaving you a little bemused but definitely intrigued.

This is the author's one-man publicity department in action – and it seems to be working. 'It's desperation, really,' Benatar tells me one sunny afternoon in Hampstead. 'If I'm not there, no books get sold and they must because I want to make a name for myself before I die. It is my ambition in life that my work should survive after I've gone.'

However, he admits that he's getting a bit fed up with the constant self-promotion. The weekend before I meet him, he sold 51 copies on Saturday but only ten in the same shop on Sunday, making him wonder if it's worth it. Still, he says, 'over the weekend 61 people who have never heard of me before now have my book and will perhaps recommend it to other people. It's not so bad.' His record so far is 128 in one day, outselling JK Rowling and John Grisham that day. All the same, he rather wishes his books would start to sell themselves.

He now has countless celebrity fans (including Emma Thompson and Joanna Lumley) and is admired by Nobel Prize winners like Doris Lessing, but he still feels he's only brushing the tail feathers of success. Benatar wrote his first novel when he was nineteen, although nothing came of it or its ten successors. Tired of each book meeting with reverberating silence, he declared to his wife that he was going to stop writing, although she knew better than to take his threat seriously. 'Writing is a compulsion,' he explains. 'It's the only talent I have. I don't understand poets who hide what they're trying to say under layers and layers of meaning - if there's something you want to say, you bend over backwards to say it, no matter what it takes.'

One day he stumbled upon a book by Pamela Hansford Johnson, the novelist, lover of Dylan Thomas and wife of C.P. Snow. 'I suddenly got the idea to write and ask her if she thought my work was any good and whether there was any point in me carrying on,' he recalls. So he sent her The Man on the Bridge. 'That's obviously a nuisance for anyone, but I was getting desperate.'

After not hearing anything from Hansford Johnson for several months, Benatar decided to call her one morning from a telephone box in Victoria Station as he made his way to Germany to look for work. As soon as she heard his name she said, 'I should have been in touch with you a long time ago. I loved your book. Of course you must go on; it deserves to be published.' He went weak at the knees.

Finding herself next to John Spears of Harper Press at a dinner party one night, Hansford Johnson recommended this new talent that had entered her life, and so Benatar won his first publishing deal. I got a tremendous advance of £400, he laughs. 'Which is actually what I got for my last novel, Letters for a Spy, and that was in 2005!'

Another break came later, when he heard John Carey, the 1982 Booker Prize chair, talking about the shortlisted nominees on the radio. 'He was saying that the judges had chosen six books but that he could name at once two others that should have been on the shortlist,' Benatar says. 'And *Wish Her Safe At Home* was one of those others.' Not one to waste an opportunity, he contacted Carey and asked if he would write a foreword for the book, which Penguin were thinking of publishing as a Modern Classic. Despite the fact that Carey agreed, describing the work as at once 'a masterpiece' and 'one of the most disturbing books I have ever read,' Penguin eventually decided against publishing the book, as did the 36 other publishing houses Benatar approached.

Frustrated, Benatar, with the help of his boyfriend John, set up his own press and began to self-publish. 'Don't self-publish unless you've been published before,' he advises. 'Because unless you've got reviews, which is what everyone immediately looks for, readers will think, "Okay, this is just some poor sad loser," and you're just going to lose money hand over fist. You'll sell it to your friends and your relatives and no one else.'

Self-publishing paid off for Benatar after he threw a launch party for the book. Returning to the scene the following morning (they weren't going to let the cases of leftover wine go to waste), Benatar caught a man on the ankle with his trolley. Employing his now-trademark sales pitch, Benatar politely directed the man over to a small display of his books. In one of those fairytale coincidences, the man with the bruised ankle revealed himself to be Edwin Franks, head of the publishing department of New York Review Books, which now publishes Wish Her Safe At Home as a Modern Classic.

Unsurprisingly, Benatar is upset by the scant regard he feels that agents, publishers and even successful authors show for burgeoning writers. He relates how he once received a rejection letter from a publisher that thanked him for the first three chapters of his manuscript and recommended he look for an agent to help 'shape his work.' He had not sent any part of his manuscript, but rather the glowing foreword written by John Carey. That the unfortunate publisher must now be kicking himself is of little comfort. 'I was able to laugh at it,' Benatar says. 'But if a first-time writer got a letter like that, it would knock his confidence out of the window. It is so irresponsible to do that.' Just as Pamela Hansford Johnson gave Benatar a hand up, he is willing to do the same, and not drop the work of young hopefuls into a specially designated wastepaper basket as did Harold Pinter.

Benatar is 73 (although you wouldn't know it to look at him) and feels that after his long, hard slog of more than half a century, he's only just beginning to achieve the recognition he believes his work deserves. However, it's comforting to know that in our youth-obsessed society, success can come later on in life and perhaps be enjoyed all the more because of that. 'I think I was getting better all the time,' Benatar says of his early failures. 'I'm quite glad I wasn't published when I was in my twenties because I'm very proud of all my books; I haven't got a favourite. I would hate to be embarrassed by anything I wrote - I want to be proud of everything.' ■

William Coles

WORKS

- Dave Cameron's Schooldays (2010)
- Lord Lucan: My Story (2009)
- The Well-Tempered Clavier (2007)

For William Coles, writing is, first and foremost, a trade. Whether this comes from his 22 years as a journalist (fifteen of which were spent at the Sun) or the seven 'turkeys' he wrote before his first book was published, I can't tell for sure. However, his tenacity and dedication are all too clear.

Coles describes the process of becoming a writer as a 'slog.' 'You have to stick at it,' he says. 'The longer you do it, you get incrementally better. I was more of a middle-ranker than a high flyer at school, but nonetheless I stuck at it and will continue to stick at it.'

Although Coles' early work never saw the light of day, these setbacks were invaluable to his career. 'I learned all my lessons from the mistakes I made. Gradually you work out what will work for you and what won't. It only took me a 150,000-word novel to appreciate that!' he laughs.

Coles found that the biggest problem he encountered when trying to write was an inability to turn off his 'internal editor,' the little voice telling him that everything he was putting down on paper was nonsense. The only way to silence this voice, he tells me, is to 'put in the hours' and 'write so much that your own inner editor switches off.'

Coles first managed to effectively silence his internal editor during the writing of his first published book, *The Well-Tempered Clavier*. He decided to write the book after a friend related the story of his first love – he had been a 17-year-old boy at boarding school and she had been his piano teacher. The inspiration for the story came when Coles cast his mind back and recalled the passionate, all-consuming jealousy synonymous with young love. 'Once I'd decided that jealousy was going to be the pulse of this little love story, it all came back to me, and suddenly I felt a little inkling of what it was to be writing in flow,' he says. 'Suddenly you are completely involved in the scene; you can picture it all and you find that the feelings that you're getting down on paper are exactly as it was.'

Another lesson that particular book taught him was to think very carefully about titles. 'It was a useless title,' he says. 'The Well-Tempered Clavier is a piece of music by Bach, which sort of binds the couple together. But I see now that it was a bit pretentious, slightly off-putting, and a lot of people don't get it – they think, What's a clavier?'

Despite this, *The Well-Tempered Clavier* helped Coles to crack another problem that had blighted his previous attempts. While being well-read is advantageous for an author, too much admiration of Dickens or Hemingway can hinder one's own voice. Coles believes he found his voice with the assistance of *The Artist's Way* by Julie Cameron. 'There are a thousand and one books out there on how to write,' he says. 'But this is one of the top-notch ones – if you're going to read any one book on the subject, read that one. If you're trying to discover an authentic voice for yourself, that's the one to go for.' ▶

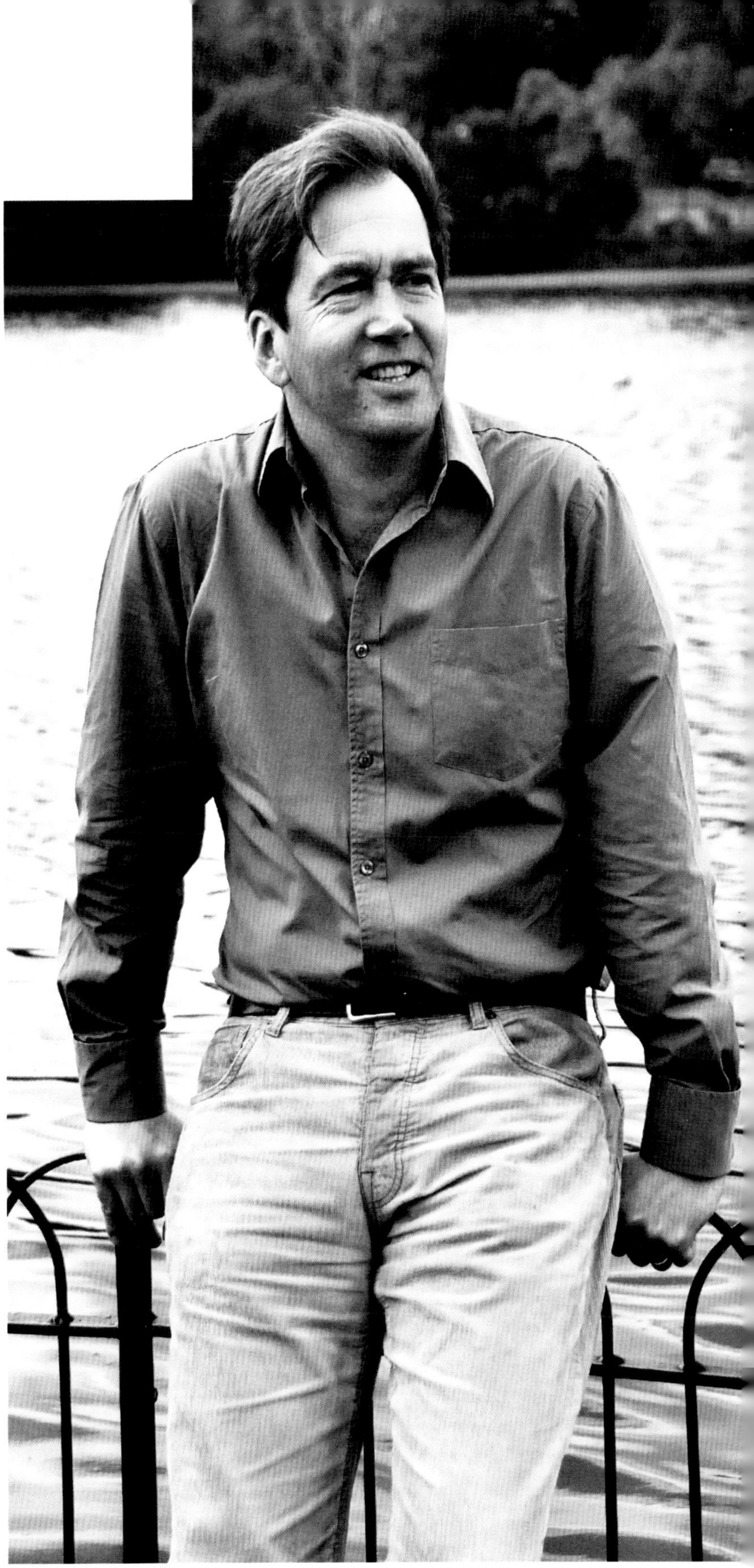

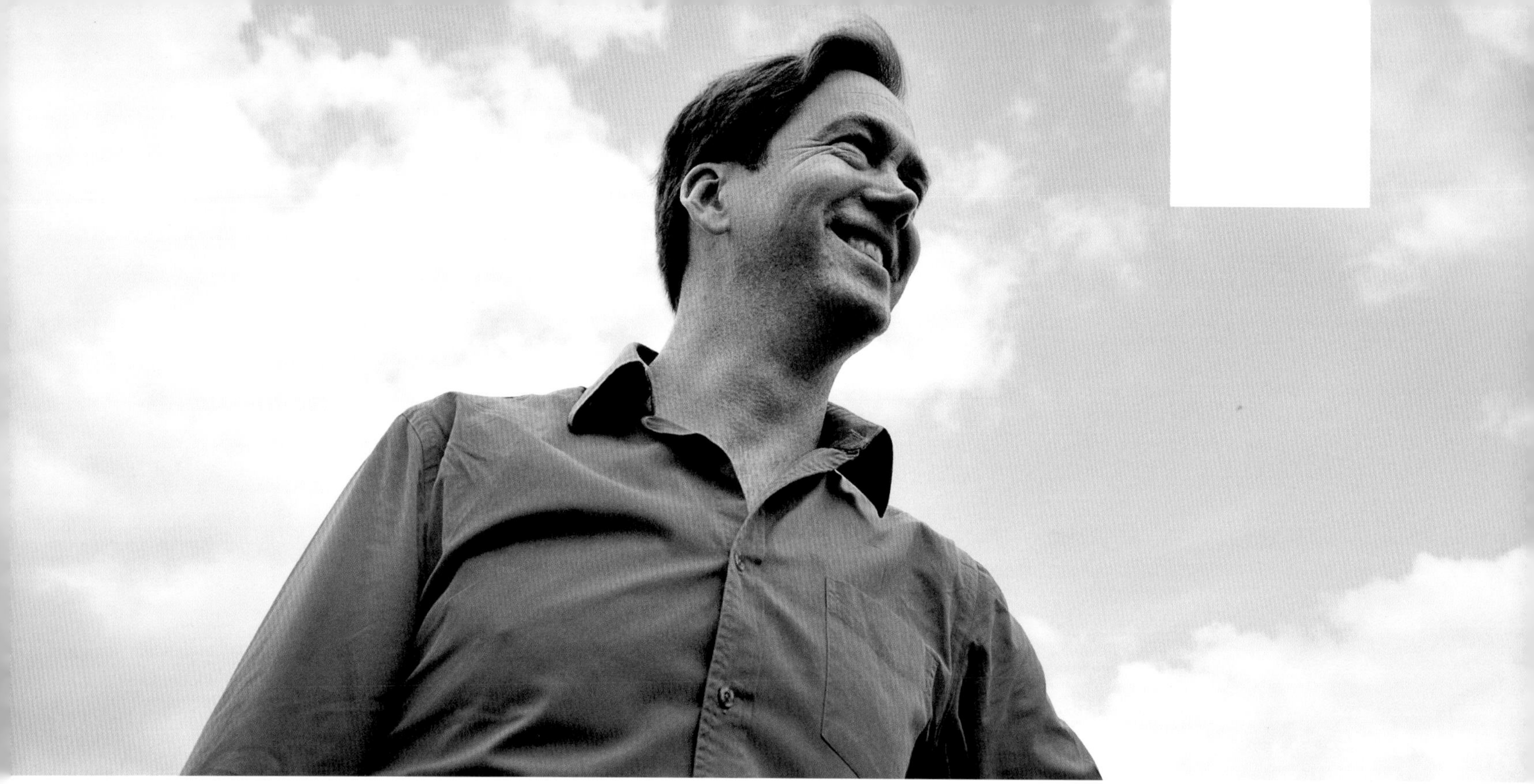

Coles particularly recommends an exercise called 'the morning pages,' which involves waking up half an hour early and writing three pages of longhand on whatever comes into your head. 'You discover seams that interest you and are going to be worth mining,' he says. Although he credits this practice with the end of his first marriage (he left some particularly contentious pages lying around; when his wife found them, she called time on the already-failing marriage), the exercise also helped him to 'break out and become comfortable' with his writing. 'One of the joys of writing is that it's very tricky to master,' he says. 'So when you do, it's a wonderful feeling.'

When it came to getting his first book published, Coles tried myriad paths. He stresses that, before sending manuscripts off to agents or publishers, writers really need six months away from their work to look at it objectively and see 'if it's any damn good.' And in order to survive rejection, which is almost inevitable, writers should move seamlessly from one project to the next. 'You just have to soldier on,' says Coles. 'There's a great tendency to write a book and to think, Here it is - now I just need to sit back and wait for the offers to come pouring in, but there's only a very small chance that it's going to be a hit, so you have to stop caring by moving on to the next project and the next project.'

Coles also recommends trying to find an agent before approaching publishers. If you send an unsolicited manuscript to a publishing house, 'it's going to go on the slush pile and you'll be lucky if the office junior reads it,' Coles warns. 'Besides, if you're in it for the long haul, you want to be writing, not cutting deals with publishers.'

Luckily, Coles enjoys a good working relationship with his publisher, who propelled him toward his most demanding writing challenge yet. Over dinner one night, Coles joked that he wanted to write something about David Cameron's Eton school days - he had been a few years above Cameron at school - and his publisher loved the idea. But this was December 2009, and if they were to get the book out by the time the election was called at the beginning of April 2010, Coles would have to write the book in just one month.

'I had no idea where it was going,' he recalls. 'There was no time to be precious about it. If I came across any structural flaws we were stuffed, because we wouldn't have enough time to deal with them.' Writing three thousand words a day every day, Coles found that the momentum carried him through. He finished the first draft of *Dave Cameron's Schooldays*, including a partial rewrite, in just three weeks. 'After about 20,000 words, I'd really nailed the voice and I went full throttle, really lampooning David Cameron,' he says. 'You don't want to get too bogged down at the start and constantly going back and fixing little things. Ideally, the project will evolve as you go along.'

'There's a slight perception that writing is arty-farty,' Coles concludes. 'But I would contend that it is a discipline and you've got to learn it, practice it and stick with it, and it can be pretty bloody boring.' As with everything that is creative and popular, he argues, there is no magic - just tenacity. 'If you think of writing as a trade, rather than dipping your pen in every now and then as the muse strikes, you will appreciate that there is a lot of spadework to be done.' He pauses and smiles. 'How boring is that?' ■

Find out more at www.wcoles.com.

Minette Walters

NOVELS

- The Chameleon's Shadow (2008)
- Chicken Feed: Quick Reads (2006)
- The Devil's Feather (2005)
- Disordered Minds (2003)
- Fox Evil (2002)
- Acid Row (2001)
- The Shape of Snakes (2000)
- The Tinder Box (1999)
- The Breaker (1998)
- The Echo (1997)
- The Dark Room (1995)
- The Scold's Bridle (1994)
- The Sculptress (1993)
- The Ice House (1992)

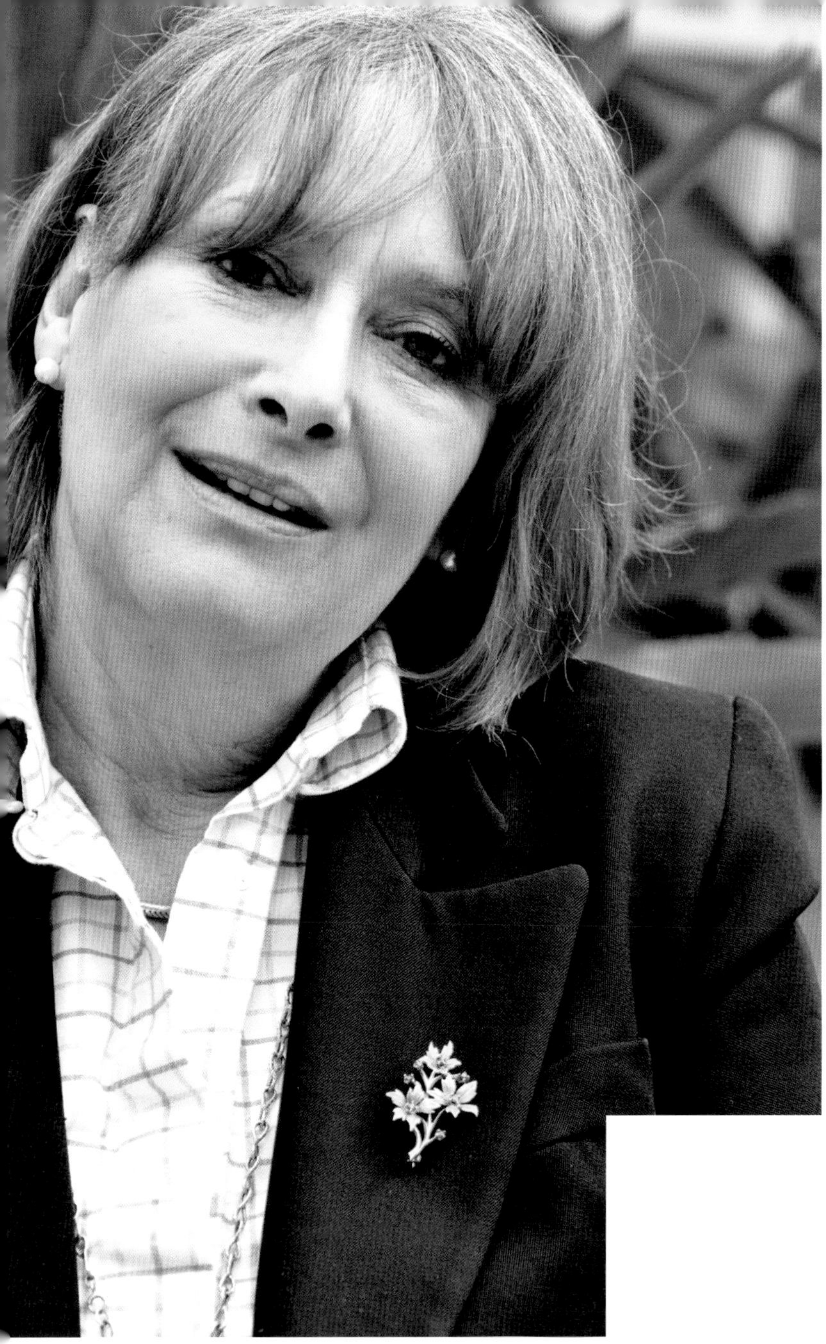

When most children are asked what they want to be when they grow up, they might say 'an astronaut' or 'a cowboy,' which they eventually grow out of as the years pass and reality sets in. Not so for Minette Walters. When she was asked, aged ten, what she wanted to be, she said 'a writer.'

Walters drew her early inspiration from Arthur Conan Doyle and Agatha Christie stories, while a school that punished lazy spelling and grammar with a sharp rap on the knuckles drew out her ability to express herself on paper. Astonishingly, Walters' talent was not spotted by her English teacher. 'She wrote to me around the time *The Scold's Bridle* came out,' Walters recalls. 'I went to see her and she was very funny. wwJilly Cooper was at the same school as me and my teacher said to me, "Do you know, if I had to pick the two girls least likely to become bestselling authors it would have been you and Jilly Cooper!"' In fact, she told Walters that she 'never saw any imagination' in her writing at all. This, Walters tells me, was because as a child she wasn't encouraged to be imaginative in her schoolwork, and it was much easier to write something boring that ticked all the boxes to avoid punishment.

Despite this, Walters is thankful for her grounding in spelling and grammar. 'It is vital to the presentation of your manuscript – if the editor is faced with lots of mistakes it will hugely put them off. They immediately get a sense, rightly or wrongly, that a person isn't really up to standard. Even if their story's great, these mistakes say that this person doesn't really understand the language they're writing in.'

At university Walters began to write creatively and produced an incredible amount of articles and plays, although, she laughs, 'I couldn't get anyone to put them on. They were a cross between Jean-Paul Sartre and Samuel Beckett and looking back they were absolute rubbish!'

Upon leaving university, she worked as a journalist but, preferring fiction to fact, eventually became the editor of a romantic fiction magazine, which gave Walters her first real glimpse of the difficulties of being a writer. 'I was reading between 200 and 400 short manuscripts a month, and out of those I'd be lucky to find four good ones.' To make up the numbers she had to put together a stable of reliable writers to write stories under assumed names; Walters herself wrote about 28 of them.

Although she 'hated' writing romance, it was wonderful practice for creating character and plot. 'Crime and romance amount to the same thing,' she advises. 'Even romance needs suspense. Half the problem with the manuscripts that were sent in was that people didn't grasp that romance requires suspense.'

After Walters married and had children, she started freelancing; however, finding time to write became almost impossible . 'It was a nightmare! If you're trying to write, just let me warn you of the row that babies make! I was not prepared for the level of yelling and demands for food, and by the time the second one arrived, it was hopeless and I just gave up totally. I didn't write anything for seven years. I threw myself into other things.'

Walters kept herself so busy - she even stood in an election - that she didn't miss writing at first. 'I think it was good to have a sort of break,' she says. 'If you're a journalist and your ambition is to do a novel, unless you have a total break from working you don't really have an incentive to give up the bread-and-butter side of writing.' ▶

However, once her youngest son started primary school, Walters suddenly had whole days stretching before her with nothing to do. It was then that she started her first book, *The Ice House*. Despite her background in romantic fiction, Walters explains, she was 'always interested in the darkness of murder stories. It's more interesting than the sparkling lightness of romance.'

The whole process took three years, from inception to publication. 'The story wasn't really ticking in the back of my mind,' she says. 'I wish it had been - it would have been a lot quicker to write.' The path to being published was also fraught with setbacks. Walters sent the manuscript to Heinemann and Random House. First, an editor at Heinemann rang her the day he received it, saying he wanted to publish it. 'I was over the moon,' Walters recalls. 'I was expecting to wait six months for any kind of response. So I rushed down to the off-license and bought a bottle of champagne to celebrate.' However, a week later the manuscript was returned in the post with a note saying that none of the other editors liked it, so they weren't going to publish it after all.

Then an editor from Random House showed interest, but he wanted rewrites. 'So I did the rewrites,' Walters says, 'and the bastard turned it down!' By this stage, she had almost finished her second novel, The Sculptress. 'I thought if I could get *The Sculptress* published, with any luck *The Ice House* might get published.' But a year later, in a wonderful twist of fate, a former assistant at Random House who remembered the manuscript and had since moved to Macmillan called Walter's agent asking to buy it. Within a few weeks, Walters had fifteen foreign publishers.

Since then, Walters has become one of the grande dames of crime fiction; her literary prizes include The Golden Dagger and The John Creasey Memorial award. Having been a judge on award panels herself, Walters is very aware that winning awards doesn't make her book the best of the year. 'I'd love to believe it was true, but it would be very foolish!' she says. 'But it's a wonderful selling tool for your next book or for the paperback edition.'

Many of her novels have been adapted for the screen. 'The quality started to go downhill a bit,' Walters says, 'which is why we decided to stop. They also wanted to make them very fast so they aired at almost the same time as the paperback came out. That's ridiculous, because if you put out an adaptation on television when the paperback is going out you're not going to sell any paperbacks' - which is where writers make most of their money. 'People assume that anything to do with television and film is megabucks,' she says, 'but it's not. And sometimes all they keep of what you wrote is the title!'

Walters, like many writers, dislikes the publicity aspect of her job. 'I love writing,' she says. 'My preferred lifestyle would be just to sit and write all day long and never have to get involved in the other side of publishing.' Even a worldwide bestseller such as Walters still needs to work the publicity circuit. 'If an author is willing to live in London and to put themselves about all the time, their profile is immediately going to go up,' she points out. 'I think that's what publishers really want these days – authors who are willing to basically attend every festival, every signing, and keep doing it. My advice to authors is to recognise that it is now required.'

For Walters, the hardest part of writing is committing ideas to paper. 'I could give you six ideas in the next five minutes, but it's all the hard graft of turning an idea into a readable 120,000 words,' she reveals. 'People love to assume that writers just sit around waiting for the muse to strike and it's just not like that. It's depressing that you can picture an entire scene in your head which works brilliantly, but to actually put that scene down on to paper could take a week or two. There are no shortcuts to writing. You have to recognise that it's hard work and you just have to dedicate yourself. Inspiration is really less important than your absolute stamina and desire to finish. I think lots of people simply lack the stamina. They write five chapters and then they give up.'

Walters finds it 'really quite entertaining' when people assume that because she writes crime novels she must have a dark, disturbed mind. To write about the darker side of the human personality, she states, 'you just have to let your imagination go.' When advising would-be crime writers, she asks them to imagine a time of extreme anger and call on that feeling. 'It works for whatever you're writing,' she says. 'You will have experienced the emotion you're trying to convey - you've just got to try and dredge up the memory of what it felt like and then put it into a different context. The more of yourself or your experiences you can put into your writing, the more authentic your story becomes.' ■

www.minettewalters.co.uk